BIG IDEAS
MATH.

BLUE

Record and Practice Journal

- Activity Recording Journal

- Activity Manipulatives

- Extra Practice Worksheets

- Fair Game Review Worksheets

- Glossary

BIG IDEAS LEARNING.

Erie, Pennsylvania

Big Ideas Learning and *Big Ideas Math* are registered trademarks of Larson Texts, Inc.

ISBN 13: 978-1-60840-234-2
ISBN 10: 1-60840-234-7

123456789-VLP-15 14 13 12 11

Contents

Chapter 1   Solving Equations

Fair Game Review Worksheets 1

1.1   Solving Simple Equations

Activity Recording Journal 3

Practice Worksheet... 6

1.2   Solving Multi-Step Equations

Activity Recording Journal 7

Practice Worksheet... 10

1.3   Solving Equations with Variables on Both Sides

Activity Recording Journal 11

Practice Worksheet... 14

1.3b   Solutions of Linear Equations

Practice Worksheet... 14A

1.4   Rewriting Equations and Formulas

Activity Recording Journal 15

Practice Worksheet... 18

1.5   Converting Units of Measure

Activity Recording Journal 19

Practice Worksheet... 22

Chapter 2   Graphing Linear Equations and Linear Systems

Fair Game Review Worksheets 23

2.1   Graphing Linear Equations

Activity Recording Journal 25

Practice Worksheet... 28

2.2   Slope of a Line

Activity Recording Journal 29

Practice Worksheet... 32

2.2b   Triangles and Slope

Practice Worksheet... 32A

2.3   Graphing Linear Equations in Slope-Intercept Form

Activity Recording Journal 33

Practice Worksheet... 36

Contents

2.4 **Graphing Linear Equations in Standard Form**

Activity Recording Journal 37

Practice Worksheet 40

2.5 **Systems of Linear Equations**

Activity Recording Journal 41

Practice Worksheet 44

2.6 **Special Systems of Linear Equations**

Activity Recording Journal 45

Practice Worksheet 48

2.7 **Solving Equations by Graphing**

Activity Recording Journal 49

Practice Worksheet 52

Chapter 3 **Writing Linear Equations and Linear Systems**

Fair Game Review Worksheets 53

3.1 **Writing Equations in Slope-Intercept Form**

Activity Recording Journal 55

Practice Worksheet 58

3.2 **Writing Equations Using a Slope and a Point**

Activity Recording Journal 59

Practice Worksheet 62

3.3 **Writing Equations Using Two Points**

Activity Recording Journal 63

Practice Worksheet 66

3.4 **Solving Real-Life Problems**

Activity Recording Journal 67

Practice Worksheet 70

3.5 **Writing Systems of Linear Equations**

Activity Recording Journal 71

Practice Worksheet 74

Chapter 4 **Functions**

Fair Game Review Worksheets 75

4.1 **Domain and Range of a Function**

Activity Recording Journal 77

Practice Worksheet 80

Contents

4.2 Discrete and Continuous Domains

Activity Recording Journal 81

Practice Worksheet 84

4.3 Linear Function Patterns

Activity Recording Journal 85

Practice Worksheet 88

4.4 Comparing Linear and Nonlinear Functions

Activity Recording Journal 89

Practice Worksheet 92

4.4b Comparing Rates

Practice Worksheet 92A

Chapter 5 Angles and Similarity

Fair Game Review Worksheets 93

5.1 Classifying Angles

Activity Recording Journal 95

Practice Worksheet 98

5.2 Angles and Sides of Triangles

Activity Recording Journal 99

Practice Worksheet 102

5.3 Angles of Polygons

Activity Recording Journal 103

Practice Worksheet 106

5.4 Using Similar Triangles

Activity Recording Journal 107

Practice Worksheet 110

5.5 Parallel Lines and Transversals

Activity Recording Journal 111

Practice Worksheet 114

Chapter 6 Square Roots and the Pythagorean Theorem

Fair Game Review Worksheets 115

6.1 Finding Square Roots

Activity Recording Journal 117

Practice Worksheet 120

Contents

6.2   The Pythagorean Theorem

Activity Recording Journal 121

Practice Worksheet 124

6.3   Approximating Square Roots

Activity Recording Journal 125

Practice Worksheet 128

6.3b   Real Numbers

Practice Worksheet 128A

6.4   Simplifying Square Roots

Activity Recording Journal 129

Practice Worksheet 132

6.5   Using the Pythagorean Theorem

Activity Recording Journal 133

Practice Worksheet 136

Chapter 7   Data Analysis and Displays

Fair Game Review Worksheets 137

7.1   Measures of Central Tendency

Activity Recording Journal 139

Practice Worksheet 142

7.2   Box-and-Whisker Plots

Activity Recording Journal 143

Practice Worksheet 146

7.3   Scatter Plots and Lines of Best Fit

Activity Recording Journal 147

Practice Worksheet 150

7.3b   Two-Way Tables

Practice Worksheet 150A

7.4   Choosing a Data Display

Activity Recording Journal 151

Practice Worksheet 154

Chapter 8   Linear Inequalities

Fair Game Review Worksheets 155

8.1   Writing and Graphing Inequalities

Activity Recording Journal 157

Practice Worksheet 160

Contents

8.2   **Solving Inequalities Using Addition or Subtraction**

Activity Recording Journal 161

Practice Worksheet.. 164

8.3   **Solving Inequalities Using Multiplication or Division**

Activity Recording Journal 165

Practice Worksheet.. 168

8.4   **Solving Multi-Step Inequalities**

Activity Recording Journal 169

Practice Worksheet.. 172

Chapter 9   **Exponents and Scientific Notation**

Fair Game Review Worksheets 173

9.1   **Exponents**

Activity Recording Journal 175

Practice Worksheet.. 178

9.2   **Product of Powers Property**

Activity Recording Journal 179

Practice Worksheet.. 182

9.3   **Quotient of Powers Property**

Activity Recording Journal 183

Practice Worksheet.. 186

9.4   **Zero and Negative Exponents**

Activity Recording Journal 187

Practice Worksheet.. 190

9.5   **Reading Scientific Notation**

Activity Recording Journal 191

Practice Worksheet.. 194

9.6   **Writing Scientific Notation**

Activity Recording Journal 195

Practice Worksheet.. 198

9.6b   **Scientific Notation**

Practice Worksheet.. 198A

Contents

Additional Topics

Fair Game Review Worksheets.. 199

Topic 1   Transformations

Practice Worksheet 201

Topic 2   Volume

Practice Worksheet 203

Glossary 205

Activity Manipulatives 233

Name_____   Date _____

Complete the statement.

1. 5 qt ≈ _____ L

2. 25 cm = _____ in.

3. 200 mL ≈ _____ cups

4. 600 grams ≈ _____ oz

5. A can of orange juice is 12 ounces. How many grams is the can of orange juice?

6. A recipe calls for 100 milliliters of water. How many cups of water does the recipe call for?

7. You buy a 5-pound bag of dog food. How many kilograms of dog food did you buy?

Name _____ Date _____

Evaluate the expression.

8. $\dfrac{1}{2} + \dfrac{2}{3}$

9. $1\dfrac{2}{5} + \dfrac{3}{8}$

10. $\dfrac{9}{10} - \dfrac{3}{5}$

11. $2\dfrac{1}{2} - 1\dfrac{1}{4}$

12. A recipe calls for $\dfrac{1}{2}$ teaspoon of salt for the batter and $\dfrac{1}{8}$ teaspoon of salt for the topping. How much salt is used in the entire recipe?

13. You have $\dfrac{3}{4}$ cup of flour. The recipe calls for $3\dfrac{1}{3}$ cups of flour. How much more flour do you need to make the recipe?

Name_____ Date_____

Essential Question How can you use inductive reasoning to discover rules in mathematics? How can you test a rule?

1 **ACTIVITY:** Sum of the Angles of a Triangle

Work with a partner. Use a protractor to measure the angles of each triangle. Complete the table to organize your results.

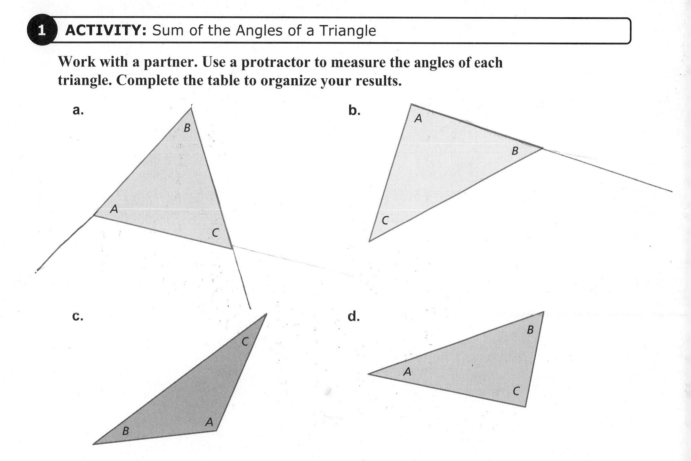

a.

b.

c.

d.

Triangle	Angle A (degrees)	Angle B (degrees)	Angle C (degrees)	A + B + C
a.	60°	60°	60°	180°
b.	90°	45°	45°	180°
c.	120°	30°	30°	180°
d.	60°	30°	90°	180°

1.1 Solving Simple Equations (continued)

2 ACTIVITY: Writing a Rule

Work with a partner. Use inductive reasoning to write and test a rule.

a. Use the completed table in Activity 1 to write a rule about the sum of the angle measures of a triangle. *It's always 180°*

b. **TEST YOUR RULE** Draw four triangles that are different from those in Activity 1. Measure the angles of each triangle. Organize your results in a table. Find the sum of the angle measures of each triangle.

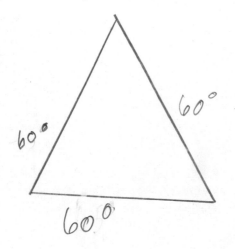

60° 60° 60°

A	B	C	
60°	60°	60°	180°

1.1 **Solving Simple Equations** (continued)

3 **ACTIVITY:** Applying Your Rule

Work with a partner. Use the rule you wrote in Activity 2 to write an equation for each triangle. Then, solve the equation to find the value of *x*. Use a protractor to check the reasonableness of your answer.

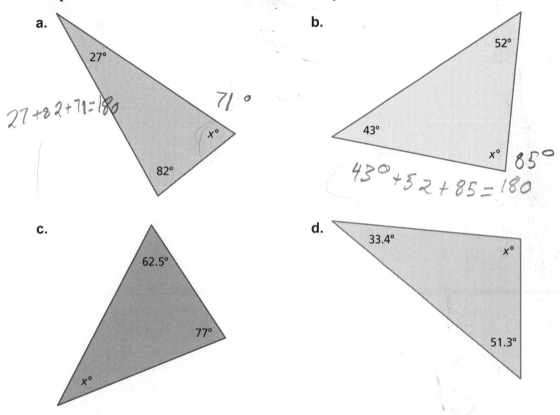

a.

27°

82°

$x°$

$27+82+71=180$ $71°$

b.

52°

43°

$x°$ $85°$

$43°+52+85=180$

c.

62.5°

77°

$x°$

d.

33.4°

$x°$

51.3°

What Is Your Answer?

4. **IN YOUR OWN WORDS** How can you use inductive reasoning to discover rules in mathematics? How can you test a rule? How can you use a rule to solve problems in mathematics?

1.1 Practice
For use after Lesson 1.1

Solve the equation. Check your solution.

1. $x + 5 = 16$

2. $11 = w - 12$

3. $\dfrac{3}{4} + z = \dfrac{5}{6}$

4. $3y = 18$

5. $\dfrac{k}{7} = 10$

6. $\dfrac{4}{5}n = \dfrac{9}{10}$

7. $x - 12 \div 6 = 9$

8. $h + |-8| = 15$

9. $1.3(2) + p = 7.9$

10. A coupon subtracts $5.16 from the price p of a shirt. You pay $15.48 for the shirt after using the coupon. Write and solve an equation to find the original price of the shirt.

11. After a party, you have $\dfrac{1}{6}$ of the cookies you made left over. There are a dozen cookies left. How many cookies did you make for the party?

Name_____ Date_____

Essential Question How can you solve a multi-step equation? How can you check the reasonableness of your solution?

1 ACTIVITY: Solving for the Angles of a Triangle

Work with a partner. Write an equation for each triangle. Solve the equation to find the value of the variable. Then find the angle measures of each triangle. Use a protractor to check the reasonableness of your answer.

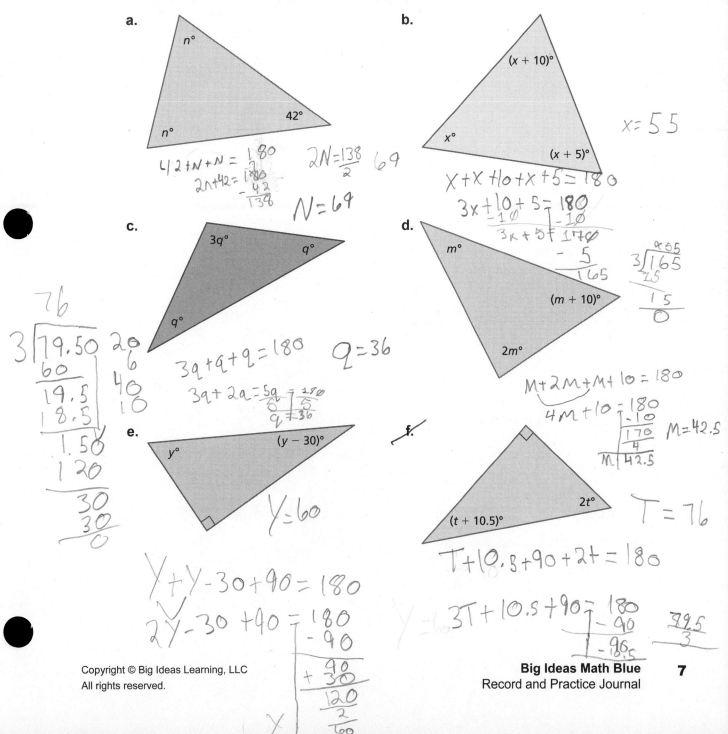

a.

$n°$

$42°$

$n°$

$42+N+N = 180$
$2n+42 = 180$
$ -42$
$ \overline{138}$

$2N=\dfrac{138}{2}$ 69

$N=69$

b.

$(x + 10)°$

$x°$

$(x + 5)°$

$x = 55$

$x+x+10+x+5=180$
$3x+10+5 = 180$
$-10 -10$
$\overline{3x+5 = 170}$
-5
$\overline{165}$

$\begin{array}{r} x55 \\ 3\overline{)165} \\ 15 \\ \hline 15 \\ 0 \end{array}$

c.

$3q°$

$q°$

$q°$

$3q+q+q=180$
$3q+2q=5q=\dfrac{180}{5}$
$q=36$

$q=36$

76

$\begin{array}{r} 76 \\ 3\overline{)79.50} \\ 60 \\ \hline 19.5 \\ 18.5 \\ \hline 1.50 \\ 1\,20 \\ \hline 30 \\ 30 \\ \hline 0 \end{array}$

$\begin{array}{r} 20 \\ 6 \\ 40 \\ 10 \end{array}$

d.

$m°$

$(m + 10)°$

$2m°$

$M+2M+M+10=180$
$4M+10 = 180$
$ -10$
$\overline{\dfrac{170}{4}}$ $M=42.5$

$m\overline{)42.5}$

$T = 76$

e.

$y°$

$(y − 30)°$

$Y=60$

$Y+Y-30+90=180$
$2Y-30+90 = 180$
$ -90$
$ + \dfrac{90}{30}$
$ \overline{\dfrac{120}{2}}$
$Y \overline{60}$

f.

$2t°$

$(t + 10.5)°$

$T+10.5+90+2t=180$
$3T+10.5+90 = 180$
$ -90$
$ -90.5$

$Y=60$ $3T+10.5+90 = 180$
$ -90$
$ -10.5$

$\dfrac{79.5}{3}$

1.2 **Solving Multi-Step Equations** (continued)

$\dfrac{3}{10}$

2 ACTIVITY: Problem Solving Strategy

Work with a partner.

The six triangles form a rectangle.

**Find the angle measures of
each triangle. Use a protractor
to check the reasonableness
of your answers.**

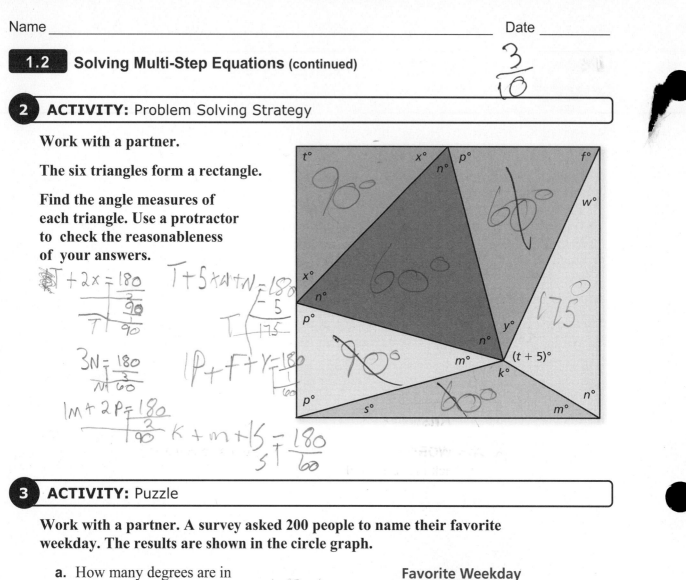

$T + 2x = 180$

$\dfrac{3}{90}$

$T \quad 90$

$T + 5x + N = 180$

$\dfrac{-5}{175}$

$T \quad 175$

$3N = 180$
$\dfrac{}{3}$
$N \quad 60$

$1P + F + Y = 180$
$\dfrac{}{60}$

$1M + 2P = 180$
$\dfrac{}{90}$

$K + m + 5 = \dfrac{180}{60}$
$5 \quad \dfrac{180}{60}$

3 ACTIVITY: Puzzle

**Work with a partner. A survey asked 200 people to name their favorite
weekday. The results are shown in the circle graph.**

  a. How many degrees are in
      each part of the circle graph? $360°$

90

  b. What percent of the people
      chose each day? $\dfrac{3}{2}x = 180$

$3 \cdot x = \dfrac{360}{3}$

$x \quad 120$

$\dfrac{3}{2}x = 180$
$\cdot 3$
540
$\cdot 2$
$x = 90$

  c. How many people chose each day?

Favorite Weekday

Tuesday
Wednesday 90
Monday $\dfrac{3}{2}x°$
$x°$
$2x°$ $3x°$
Friday
Thursday 120

1.2 **Solving Multi-Step Equations** (continued)

    d. Organize your results in a table.

What Is Your Answer?

    4. IN YOUR OWN WORDS How can you solve a multi-step equation? How can you check the reasonableness of your solution?

Name _____ Date _____

Solve the equation. Check your solution.

1. $3x - 11 = 22$

2. $24 - 10b = 9$

3. $2.4z + 1.2z - 6.5 = 0.7$

4. $\frac{3}{4}w - \frac{1}{2}w - 4 = 12$

5. $2(a + 7) - 7 = 9$

6. $20 + 8(q - 11) = -12$

7. Find the width of the rectangular prism when the surface area is 208 square centimeters.

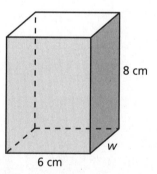

8. The amount of money in your savings account after m months is represented by $A = 135m + 225$. After how many months do you have $765 in your savings account?

Name_____ Date_____

Essential Question How can you solve an equation that has variables on both sides?

1 **ACTIVITY:** Perimeter and Area

Work with a partner. Each figure has the unusual property that the value of its perimeter (in feet) is equal to the value of its area (in square feet).

- Write an equation (value of perimeter = value of area) for each figure.
- Solve each equation for *x*.
- Use the value of *x* to find the perimeter and area of each figure.
- Check your solution by comparing the value of the perimeter and the value of the area of each figure.

a.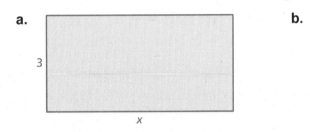

b.

c.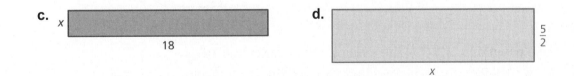

d.

1.3 **Solving Equations with Variables on Both Sides** (continued)

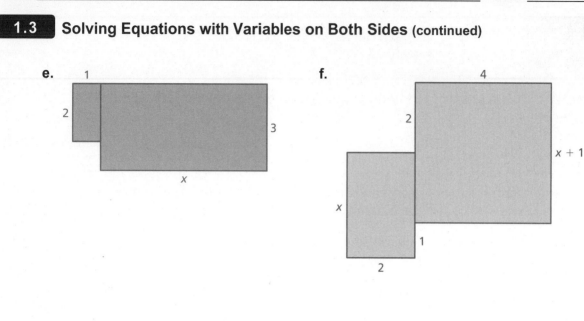

e.

f.

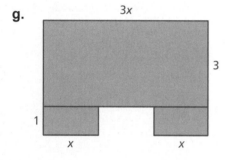

g.

---

2 **ACTIVITY:** Surface Area and Volume

Work with a partner. Each solid on the next page has the unusual property
that the value of its surface area (in square inches) is equal to the value of
its volume (in cubic inches).

- Write an equation (value of surface area = value of volume) for
  each figure.

- Solve each equation for *x*.

- Use the value of *x* to find the surface area and volume of each
  figure.

- Check your solution by comparing the value of the surface area
  and the value of the volume of each figure.

1.3 **Solving Equations with Variables on Both Sides** (continued)

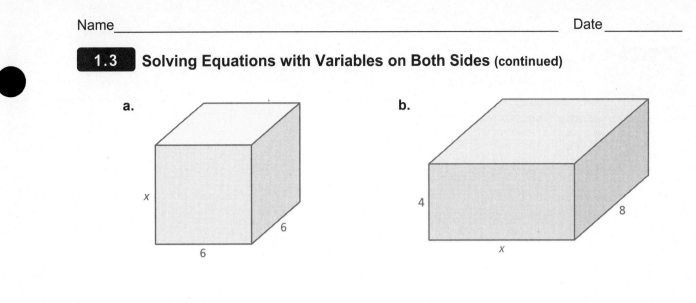

a.

b.

---

3 **ACTIVITY:** Puzzle

Work with a partner. The two triangles are similar. The perimeter of the larger triangle is 150% of the perimeter of the smaller triangle. Find the dimensions of each triangle.

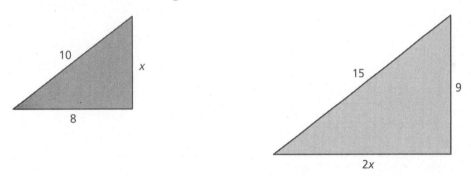

What Is Your Answer?

4. **IN YOUR OWN WORDS** How can you solve an equation that has variables on both sides? Write an equation that has variables on both sides. Solve the equation.

1.3 Practice
For use after Lesson 1.3

Solve the equation. Check your solution.

1. $x + 16 = 9x$

2. $4y - 70 = 12y + 2$

3. $5(p + 6) = 8p$

4. $3(g - 7) = 2(10 + g)$

5. $1.8 + 7n = 9.5 - 4n$

6. $\dfrac{3}{7}w - 11 = -\dfrac{4}{7}w$

7. One movie club charges a $100 membership fee and $10 for each movie. Another club charges no membership fee but movies cost $15 each. Write and solve an equation to find the number of movies you need to buy for the cost of each movie club to be the same.

8. Thirty percent of all the students in a school are in a play. All students except for 140 are in the play. How many students are in the school?

Name_____ Date_____

1.3b Practice
For use after Lesson 1.3b

Solve the equation.

1. $x = x + 3$

2. $-4x = -2 - 4x$

3. $7x + 5 = 7x - 1$

4. $-3(2x + 1) = -2(3x - 4)$

5. $2x + 4 = 2x + 4$

6. $-5(x + 2) = -5x - 10$

Name _____ Date _____

7. $4(-2x + 5) = -2(4x + 5)$

8. $\frac{1}{6}(36 - 24x) = \frac{2}{3}(9 - 6x)$

9. $-7x - 9 = -5x + 7$

10. $-5(x + 2.5) = -4x - 7.5$

11. Are there any values of x for which the perimeters of the figures are the same? Explain.

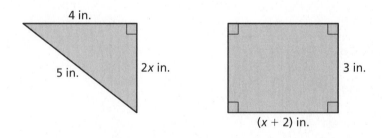

Name_____ Date_____

1.4 Rewriting Equations and Formulas
For use with Activity 1.4

Essential Question How can you use a formula for one measurement to write a formula for a different measurement?

---

1 ACTIVITY: Using Perimeter and Area Formulas

Work with a partner.

a. • Write a formula for the perimeter P of a rectangle.

• Solve the formula for w.

• Use the new formula to find the width of the rectangle.

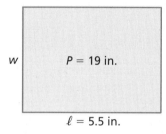

w $P = 19$ in.

$\ell = 5.5$ in.

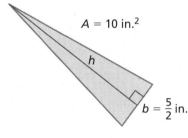

$A = 10$ in.^{2}

h

$b = \dfrac{5}{2}$ in.

b. • Write a formula for the area A of a triangle.

• Solve the formula for h.

• Use the new formula to find the height of the triangle.

c. • Write a formula for the circumference C of a circle.

• Solve the formula for r.

• Use the new formula to find the radius of the circle.

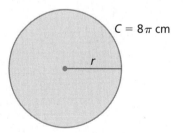

$C = 8\pi$ cm

r

1.4 **Rewriting Equations and Formulas** (continued)

- Write a formula for the area *A.*
- Solve the formula for *h.*
- Use the new formula to find the height.

d.

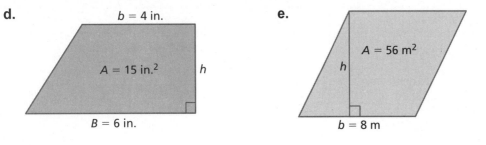

b = 4 in.

A = 15 in.²   *h*

B = 6 in.

e.

A = 56 m²

h

b = 8 m

---

2 **ACTIVITY:** Using Volume Formulas

Work with a partner.

a.
- Write a formula for the volume *V* of a prism.
- Solve the formula for *h.*
- Use the new formula to find the height of the prism.

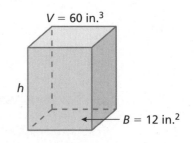

V = 60 in.³

h

B = 12 in.²

1.4   **Rewriting Equations and Formulas** (continued)

- Write a formula for the volume *V*.
- Solve the formula for *B*.
- Use the new formula to find the area of the base.

b.

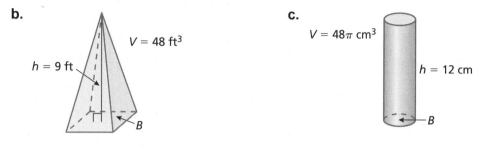

   $V = 48$ ft^3

$h = 9$ ft

B

c.

$V = 48\pi$ cm^3

$h = 12$ cm

B

d.
- Write a formula for the volume *V* of a cone.
- Solve the formula for *h*.
- Use the new formula to find the height of the cone.

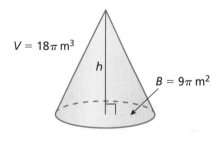

$V = 18\pi$ m^3

h

$B = 9\pi$ m^2

What Is Your Answer?

3. **IN YOUR OWN WORDS** How can you use a formula for one measurement to write a formula for a different measurement? Give an example that is different from the examples on these three pages.

Name _____ Date _____

Solve the equation for y.

1. $2x + y = -9$

2. $4x - 10y = 12$

3. $13 = \dfrac{1}{6}y + 2x$

Solve the equation for the bold variable.

4. $V = \ell wh$

5. $f = \dfrac{1}{2}(\boldsymbol{r} + 6.5)$

6. $S = 2\pi r^2 + 2\pi r\boldsymbol{h}$

7. The formula for the area of a triangle is $A = \dfrac{1}{2}bh$.

   a. Solve the formula for h.

   b. Use the new formula to find the value of h.

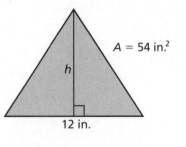

$A = 54$ in.²

h

12 in.

Name_____ Date_____

1.5 Converting Units of Measure
For use with Activity 1.5

Essential Question How can you convert from one measurement system to another?

1 ACTIVITY: Converting Units of Measure

Work with a partner. Complete the table. Describe the pattern in the completed table.

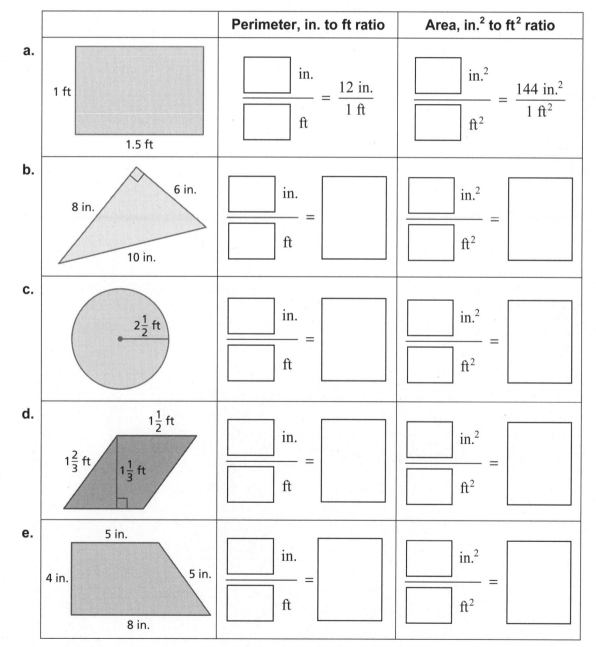

		Perimeter, in. to ft ratio	Area, in.² to ft² ratio
a.	1 ft, 1.5 ft	$\dfrac{\boxed{} \text{ in.}}{\boxed{} \text{ ft}} = \dfrac{12 \text{ in.}}{1 \text{ ft}}$	$\dfrac{\boxed{} \text{ in.}^2}{\boxed{} \text{ ft}^2} = \dfrac{144 \text{ in.}^2}{1 \text{ ft}^2}$
b.	8 in., 6 in., 10 in.	$\dfrac{\boxed{} \text{ in.}}{\boxed{} \text{ ft}} = \boxed{}$	$\dfrac{\boxed{} \text{ in.}^2}{\boxed{} \text{ ft}^2} = \boxed{}$
c.	$2\frac{1}{2}$ ft	$\dfrac{\boxed{} \text{ in.}}{\boxed{} \text{ ft}} = \boxed{}$	$\dfrac{\boxed{} \text{ in.}^2}{\boxed{} \text{ ft}^2} = \boxed{}$
d.	$1\frac{1}{2}$ ft, $1\frac{2}{3}$ ft, $1\frac{1}{3}$ ft	$\dfrac{\boxed{} \text{ in.}}{\boxed{} \text{ ft}} = \boxed{}$	$\dfrac{\boxed{} \text{ in.}^2}{\boxed{} \text{ ft}^2} = \boxed{}$
e.	5 in., 4 in., 5 in., 8 in.	$\dfrac{\boxed{} \text{ in.}}{\boxed{} \text{ ft}} = \boxed{}$	$\dfrac{\boxed{} \text{ in.}^2}{\boxed{} \text{ ft}^2} = \boxed{}$

1.5 Converting Units of Measure (continued)

2 ACTIVITY: Comparing Units of Measure

Work with a partner. Name the units for each pair of "rulers."

a.

b.

c.

1.5 **Converting Units of Measure** (continued)

3 **ACTIVITY:** Puzzle

Who is correct, Fred or Sam? Explain your reasoning.

John said, "We left camp this morning, and walked 1 mile due south. Then, we saw a polar bear and turned due east and ran 1 kilometer. Finally, we turned due north and walked 1 mile and ended back at camp."

Fred said, "That is not possible!"

Sam explained, "Yes it is. And I know exactly where the camp was."

What Is Your Answer?

4. **IN YOUR OWN WORDS** How can you convert from one measurement system to another? The examples on these three pages are measurements of length and area. Describe a conversion between two types of temperature units.

Name _____ Date _____

Complete the statement.

1. 3 m ≈ _____ ft

2. 32 cm ≈ _____ in.

3. 16 qt ≈ _____ L

4. $\dfrac{50 \text{ mi}}{\text{h}} \approx \dfrac{\boxed{} \text{ km}}{\text{h}}$

5. $\dfrac{25 \text{ gal}}{\text{min}} = \dfrac{\boxed{} \text{ qt}}{\text{sec}}$

6. $\dfrac{1000 \text{ m}}{\text{sec}} = \dfrac{\boxed{} \text{ km}}{\text{min}}$

7. 20 in.^{2} ≈ _____ ft^2

8. 50 ft^2 ≈ _____ yd^2

9. 50 m^3 = _____ cm^3

10. Your doctor prescribes you to take 400 milligrams of medicine every 8 hours. How many ounces of medicine do you take in a day?

11. In Canada, a speed limit is 100 kilometers per hour. What is the speed limit in miles per hour?

Chapter 2 — Fair Game Review

Evaluate the expression when $x = \dfrac{1}{2}$ and $y = -5$.

1. $-2xy$

2. $4x^2 - 3y$

3. $\dfrac{10y}{12x + 4}$

4. $11x - 8(x - y)$

Evaluate the expression when $a = -9$ and $b = -4$.

5. $3ab$

6. $a^2 - 2(b + 12)$

7. $\dfrac{4b^2}{3b - 7}$

8. $7b^2 + 5(ab - 6)$

9. You go to the movies with five friends. Two of you buy a ticket and a bag of popcorn. The rest of your friends buy just one ticket. The expression $4x + 2(x + y)$ represents the situation. Evaluate the expression when tickets cost \$7.25 and a bag of popcorn costs \$3.25.

Name _____ Date _____

Chapter 2 **Fair Game Review** (continued)

Use the graph to answer the question.

10. Write the ordered pair that corresponds to Point *D*.

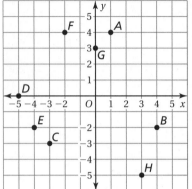

11. Write the ordered pair that corresponds to Point *H*.

12. Which point is located at $(-2, 4)$?

13. Which point is located at $(0, 3)$?

14. Which point(s) are located in Quadrant IV?

15. Which point(s) are located in Quadrant III?

Plot the point.

16. $(3, -1)$

17. $(0, 2)$

18. $(-5, -4)$

19. $(-1, 0)$

20. $(-2, 3)$

Graphing Linear Equations
For use with Activity 2.1

Essential Question How can you recognize a linear equation? How can you draw its graph?

1 **ACTIVITY:** Graphing a Linear Equation

Work with a partner.

a. Use the equation $y = \frac{1}{2}x + 1$
to complete the table. (Choose any two x-values and find the y-values).

	Solution Points		
x	0	4	1
$y = \frac{1}{2}x + 1$	1	3	$1\frac{1}{2}$

b. Write the two ordered pairs given by the table. These are called **solution points** of the equation.

from John *Coonie hiq*

c. Plot the two solution points. Draw a line *exactly* through the two points.

d. Find a different point on the line. Check that this point is a solution (-20) point of the equation $y = \frac{1}{2}x + 1$.

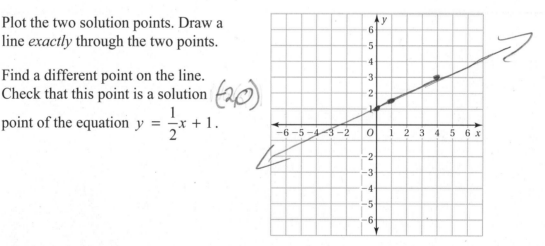

e. **GENERALIZE** Do you think it is true that *any* point on the line is a solution point of the equation $y = \frac{1}{2}x + 1$? Explain. Yes

2.1   **Graphing Linear Equations** (continued)

f. Choose five additional *x*-values for the table. (Choose positive and negative *x*-values.) Plot the five corresponding solution points on the previous page. Does each point lie on the line?

	Solution Points				
x	1	0	2	3	4
$y = \frac{1}{2}x + 1$	$1\frac{1}{2}$	1	2	$2\frac{1}{2}$	3

g. **GENERALIZE** Do you think it is true that *any* solution point of the equation $y = \frac{1}{2}x + 1$ is a point on the line? Explain. *Yes*

h. **THE MEANING OF A WORD** Why is $y = ax + b$ called a *linear equation*?

So you add #'s

---

2   **HISTORY:** Analytic Geometry

Rene Descartes was a French philosopher, scientist, and mathematician.

Up until the time of Descartes, *algebra* and *geometry* were separate fields of mathematics. Descartes's invention of the coordinate plane was of huge importance to mathematics. For the first time, people could "see" solutions of equations. No longer did people have to work with algebra from a purely symbolic point of view.

René Descartes (1596–1650)

2.1 Graphing Linear Equations (continued)

Descartes's combination of geometry and algebra is called *analytic* (or algebraic) *geometry*. One of the main discoveries in analytic geometry is that all of the important types of graphs (lines, parabolas, circles, ellipses, and so on) can be represented by simple algebraic equations.

Within a few dozen years, other mathematicians were able to discover all of *calculus*, a field of mathematics that is of great value in business, science, and engineering.

In this book, you will study lines. In Algebra 1 and Algebra 2, you will study many other types of equations.

Line: $y = ax + b$ Parabola: $y = ax^2 + b$ Circle: $x^2 + y^2 = r^2$

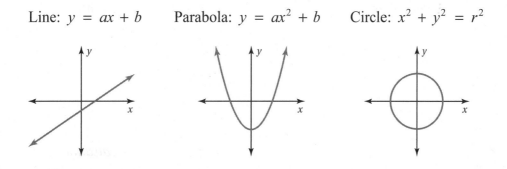

What Is Your Answer?

3. **IN YOUR OWN WORDS** How can you recognize a linear equation? How can you draw its graph? Write an equation that is linear. Write an equation that is *not* linear. By seeing if you need to Fill in the blanks

4. Are you a visual learner? Most people can learn mathematics more easily when they see "pictures" of the mathematics. Why do you think Descartes's invention was important to mathematics? So we can understand better

Name _____ Date _____

Graph the linear equation.

1. $y = 4$

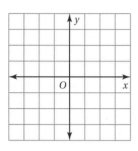

2. $y = -\dfrac{1}{3}x$

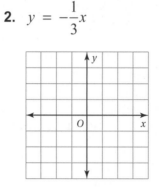

Solve for _y_. Then graph the equation.

3. $y + 2x = 3$

4. $2y - 3x = 1$

5. The equation $y = 2x + 4$ represents the cost y (in dollars) of renting a movie after x days of late charges.

   a. Graph the equation.

   b. Use the graph to determine how much it costs after 3 days of late charges.

Name_____ Date _____

2.2 Slope of a Line
For use with Activity 2.2

Essential Question How can the slope of a line be used to describe the line?

Slope is the rate of change between any two points on a line. It is the measure of the *steepness* of the line.

To find the slope of a line, find the ratio of the change in y (vertical change) to the change in x (horizontal change).

$$\text{slope} = \frac{\text{change in } y}{\text{change in } x}$$

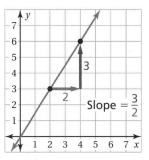

---

1 **ACTIVITY:** Finding the Slope of a Line

Work with a partner. Find the slope of each line using two methods.

Method 1: Use the two black points.

Method 2: Use the two gray points.

Do you get the same slope using each method?

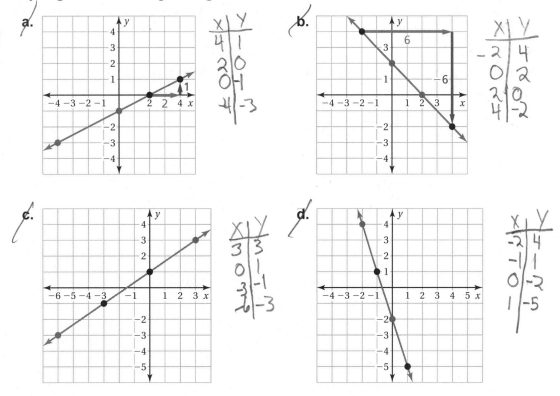

Name _____ Date _____

2 **ACTIVITY:** Drawing Lines with Given Slopes

Work with a partner.

- Draw a line through the black point using the given slope.
- Draw a line through the gray point using the given slope.
- What do you notice about the two lines?

a. Slope $= 2$

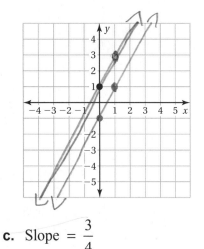

b. Slope $= -\dfrac{1}{2}$

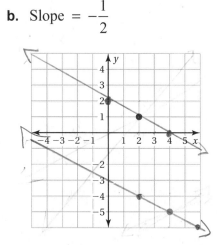

c. Slope $= \dfrac{3}{4}$

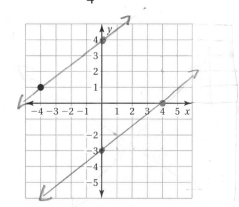

d. Slope $= -2$

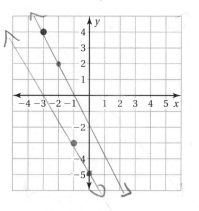

What Is Your Answer?

3. IN YOUR OWN WORDS How can the slope of a line be used to describe the line? Where it is on the Graph

2.2b **Practice**
For use after Lesson 2.2b

Tell whether the two right triangles are similar. Explain your reasoning.

1.

2.

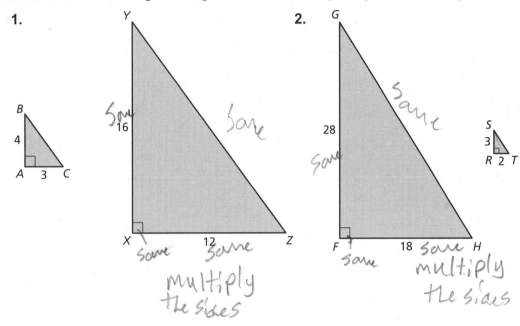

3. The graph shows similar right triangles drawn using pairs of points on a line.

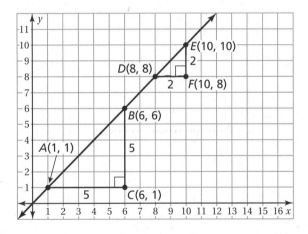

a. For each triangle, find the ratio of the length of the vertical leg to the length of the horizontal leg. They are not the same

$$\frac{2}{5}$$

b. Relate the ratios in part (a) to the slope of the line.

$$1 \cdot \frac{2}{5} = 1\frac{2}{5}$$

Name _____ Date _____

4. Consider the line shown in the graph.

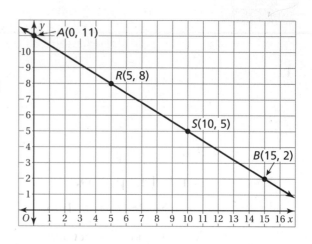

a. Draw two triangles that show the rise and the run of the line using points A and B and points R and S.

b. Use the triangles to find the slope of the line.

c. Repeat parts (a) and (b) using different pairs of points.

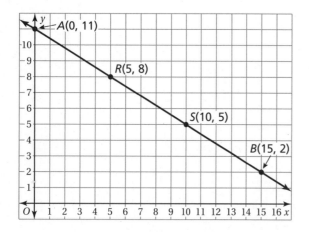

Name_____ Date_____

2.3 Graphing Linear Equations in Slope-Intercept Form
For use with Activity 2.3

Essential Question How can you describe the graph of the equation $y = mx + b$?

1 ACTIVITY: Finding Slopes and y-Intercepts

Work with a partner.

- **Graph the equation.**
- **Find the slope of the line.**
- **Find the point where the line crosses the y-axis.**

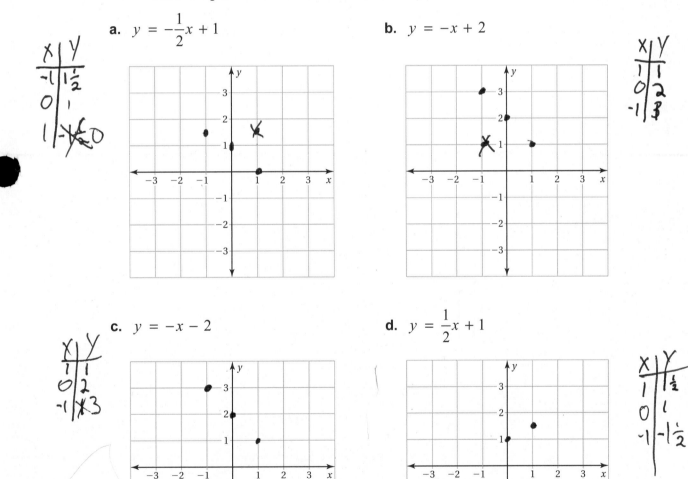

a. $y = -\dfrac{1}{2}x + 1$

X	Y
-1	$1\frac{1}{2}$
0	1
1	-½ ⟶ 0

b. $y = -x + 2$

X	Y
1	1
0	2
-1	3

c. $y = -x - 2$

X	Y
1	1
0	2
-1	×3

d. $y = \dfrac{1}{2}x + 1$

X	Y
1	1½
0	1
-1	-1½

Name _____ Date _____

Inductive Reasoning

Work with a partner. Graph each equation. Then complete the table.

	Equation	Description of Graph	Slope of Graph	Point of Intersection with *y*-axis
1a	2. $y = -\frac{1}{2}x + 1$	linear	P	0, 1
1b	3. $y = -x + 2$	linear	P	0, 2
1c	4. $y = -x - 2$	linear	N	0, -2
1d	5. $y = \frac{1}{2}x + 1$	linear	P	0, 1²⁄₂
	6. $y = x + 2$	linear	1	0, 2
	7. $y = x - 2$	linear	1	0, -1
	8. $y = \frac{1}{2}x - 1$	linear	1½	0, ½
	9. $y = -\frac{1}{2}x - 1$	linear	1½	0, 1½
	10. $y = 3x + 2$	linear	3	0, 5
	11. $y = 3x - 2$	linear	3	0, -1
	12. $y = -2x + 3$	linear	-2	0, 1

Name_____ Date_____

What Is Your Answer?

13. **IN YOUR OWN WORDS** How can you describe the graph of the equation $y = mx + b$?

    a. How does the value of m affect the graph of the equation?

    b. How does the value of b affect the graph of the equation?

    c. Check your answers to parts (a) and (b) with three equations that are not in the table.

14. Why is $y = mx + b$ called the "slope-intercept" form of the equation of a line?

Name _____ Date _____

Find the slope and *y*-intercept of the graph of the linear equation.

1. $y = -3x + 9$

2. $y = 4 - \dfrac{2}{5}x$

3. $6 + y = 8x$

Graph the linear equation. Identify the *x*-intercept.

4. $y = \dfrac{2}{3}x + 6$

5. $y - 10 = -5x$

6. The equation $y = -90x + 1440$ represents the time (in minutes) left after x games of a tournament.

   a. Graph the equation.

   b. Interpret the *x*-intercept and slope.

Name_____ Date_____

2.4 Graphing Linear Equations in Standard Form
For use with Activity 2.4

Essential Question How can you describe the graph of the equation $ax + by = c$?

1 ACTIVITY: Using a Table to Plot Points

Work with a partner. You sold a total of $16 worth of tickets to a school concert. You lost track of how many of each type of ticket you sold.

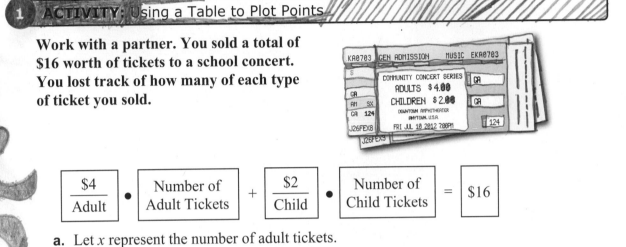

$$\frac{\$4}{\text{Adult}} \cdot \boxed{\text{Number of Adult Tickets}} + \frac{\$2}{\text{Child}} \cdot \boxed{\text{Number of Child Tickets}} = \$16$$

a. Let x represent the number of adult tickets.
   Let y represent the number of child tickets.
   Write an equation that relates x and y.

b. Complete the table showing the different combinations of tickets you might have sold.

Number of Adult Tickets, x	1	3	4	2	0
Number of Child Tickets, y	6	2	0	4	8

c. Plot the points from the table. Describe the pattern formed by the points.
   Negative slope

small Bizare

d. If you remember how many adult tickets you sold, can you determine how many child tickets you sold? Explain your reasoning. Yes because each child ticket goes down two

# of child tickets

# of Adult tickets

Name _____ Date _____

2.4 Graphing Linear Equations in Standard Form (continued)

2 ACTIVITY: Rewriting an Equation

Work with a partner. You sold a
total of $16 worth of cheese. You
forgot how many pounds of each
type of cheese you sold.

CHEESE FOR SALE
Swiss: $4/lb   Cheddar: $2/lb

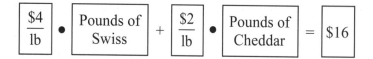

$$\boxed{\frac{\$4}{lb}} \cdot \boxed{\begin{array}{c}\text{Pounds of}\\\text{Swiss}\end{array}} + \boxed{\frac{\$2}{lb}} \cdot \boxed{\begin{array}{c}\text{Pounds of}\\\text{Cheddar}\end{array}} = \boxed{\$16}$$

a. Let x represent the number of pounds of Swiss cheese.
Let y represent the number of pounds of Cheddar cheese.
Write an equation that relates x and y.

$$16 = 4x + 2y$$

b. Write the equation in slope-intercept form. Then graph the equation.

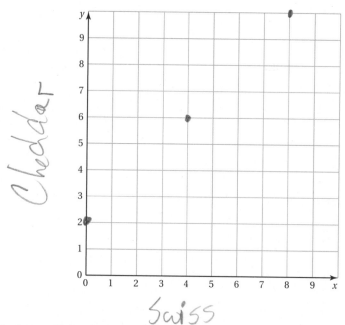

38 **Big Ideas Math Blue**
Record and Practice Journal

Name _____ Date _____

2.4 **Graphing Linear Equations in Standard Form** (continued)

What Is Your Answer?

3. **IN YOUR OWN WORDS** How can you describe the graph of the equation
   $ax + by = c$?

   A is the x axis
   B is the y axis
   C is the Y intercept

4. Activities 1 and 2 show two different methods for graphing $ax + by = c$.
   Describe the two methods. Which method do you prefer? Explain.

   I it makes it easier to look at
   and do the graph. You only have
   to look at the Data Table

5. Write a real-life problem that is similar to those shown in Activities 1 and 2.

   X Epresents the amount of people like
   hockey
   Y is the amount that like Football

Name _____ Date _____

2.4 Practice
For use after Lesson 2.4

Write the linear equation in slope-intercept form.

1. $2x - y = 7$

2. $\frac{1}{4}x + y = -\frac{2}{7}$

3. $3x - 5y = -20$

Graph the linear equation using intercepts.

4. $2x - 3y = 12$

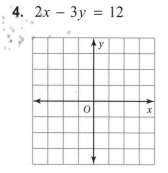

5. $x + 9y = -27$

6. You go shopping and buy x shirts for $12 and y jeans for $28. The total spent is $84.

   a. Write an equation in standard form that models how much money you spent.

   b. Graph the equation and interpret the intercepts.

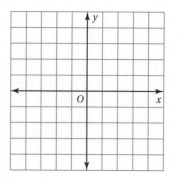

2.5 Systems of Linear Equations
For use with Activity 2.5

Essential Question How can you solve a system of linear equations?

1 ACTIVITY: Writing a System of Linear Equations

Work with a partner.

Your family starts a bed-and-breakfast in your home. You spend $500 fixing up a bedroom to rent. Your cost for food and utilities is $10 per night. Your family charges $60 per night to rent the bedroom.

a. Write an equation that represents your costs.

| Cost, C (in dollars) | = | $10 per night | $\cdot$ | Number of nights, x | + | $500 |

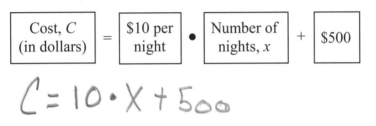

$$C = 10 \cdot X + 500$$

b. Write an equation that represents your revenue (income).

| Revenue, R (in dollars) | = | $60 per night | $\cdot$ | Number of nights, x |

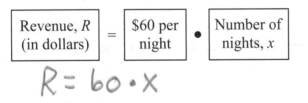

$$R = 60 \cdot X$$

c. A set of two (or more) linear equations is called a **system of linear equations**. Write the system of linear equations for this problem.

2.5 **Systems of Linear Equations** (continued)

2 **ACTIVITY:** Using a Table to Solve a System

Use the cost and revenue equations from Activity 1 to find how many nights
you need to rent the bedroom before you recover the cost of fixing up the
bedroom. This is the *break-even point* for your business.

a. Complete the table.

x	0	1	2	3	4	5	6	7	8	9	10	11
C	500	510	520	530	540	550	560	570	580	590	600	610
R	0	60	120	180	240	300	360	420	480	540	600	660

b. How many nights do you need to rent the bedroom before you break even?

10 times

3 **ACTIVITY:** Using a Graph to Solve a System

a. Graph the cost equation from Activity 1.

b. In the same coordinate plane, graph
the revenue equation from Activity 1.

R,C

c. Find the point of intersection of the
two graphs. The *x*-value of this point
is the number of nights you need to
rent the bedroom to break even.

10 nights

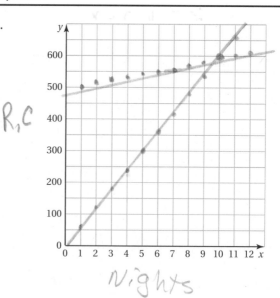

Nights

2.6 Special Systems of Linear Equations (continued)

e. Does each solution in the table satisfy *both* clues?

f. What can you conclude? How many solutions does the puzzle have? How can you describe them?

What Is Your Answer?

4. IN YOUR OWN WORDS Can a system of linear equations have no solution? Can a system of linear equations have many solutions? Give examples to support your answers.

2.6 Practice
For use after Lesson 2.6

Solve the system of linear equations.

1. $y = 2x - 5$

   $y = 2x + 7$

2. $3x + 4y = -10$

   $y = -\dfrac{3}{4}x - \dfrac{5}{2}$

3. $y = x + 6$

   $2x + y = 9$

4. $x - y = 8$

   $2y = 2x - 16$

5. You start reading a book for your literature class two days before your friend. You both read 10 pages per night. A system of linear equations that represents this situation is $y = 10x + 20$ and $y = 10x$. Will your friend finish the book before you? Explain.

6. You and a friend buy music from different online stores. The system of linear equations represents the total amount spent on x songs and y albums. Both of you buy the same number of albums. Compare the number of songs each of you buy.

   $\boxed{\begin{aligned} 0.95x + 10y &= 39.5 \\ 1.9x + 20y &= 79 \end{aligned}}$

1,

Name_____ Date_____

Essential Question How can you use a system of linear equations to solve an equation that has variables on both sides?

You learned how to use algebra to solve equations with variables on both sides. Another way is by using a system of linear equations.

1 ACTIVITY: Solving a System of Linear Equations

Work with a partner. Find the solution of $2x - 1 = -\dfrac{1}{2}x + 4$.

a. Use the left side of the equation to write one linear equation. Then, use the right side to write another linear equation.

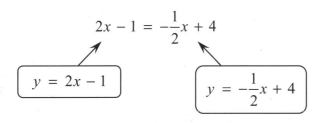

$$2x - 1 = -\frac{1}{2}x + 4$$

$$y = 2x - 1$$

$$y = -\frac{1}{2}x + 4$$

b. Sketch the graphs of the two linear equations. Find the x-value of the point of intersection.

The x-value is the solution of $2x - 1 = -\dfrac{1}{2}x + 4$.

Check the solution.

c. Explain why this "graphical method" works.

2 ACTIVITY: Using a Graphing Calculator

Use a graphing calculator to graph the two linear equations.

$$y = 2x - 1$$

$$y = -\frac{1}{2}x + 4$$

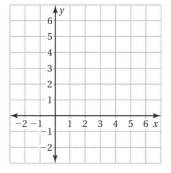

The steps used to enter the equations depend on the calculator model that you have.

2.7 **Solving Equations by Graphing** (continued)

3 **ACTIVITY:** Using a System of Linear Equations

Work with a partner. Solve the equation using two methods.

- **Method 1:** Use an algebraic method.

- **Method 2:** Use a graphical method.

- Is the solution the same using both methods?

a. $\dfrac{1}{2}x + 4 = -\dfrac{1}{4}x + 1$

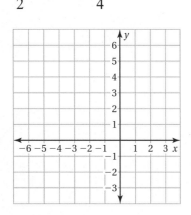

b. $\dfrac{2}{3}x + 4 = \dfrac{1}{3}x + 3$

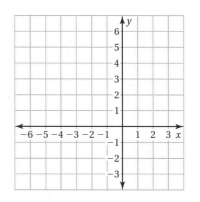

c. $-\dfrac{2}{3}x - 1 = \dfrac{1}{3}x - 4$

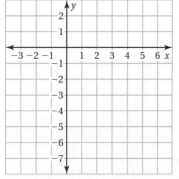

d. $\dfrac{4}{5}x + \dfrac{7}{5} = 3x - 3$

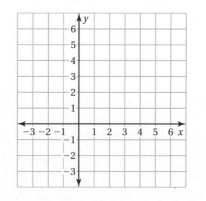

2.7 **Solving Equations by Graphing** (continued)

What Is Your Answer?

4. **IN YOUR OWN WORDS** How can you use a system of linear equations to solve an equation that has variables on both sides? Give an example that is different from those in Activities 1 and 3.

5. Describe three ways in which Rene Descartes's invention of the coordinate plane allows you to solve algebraic problems graphically.

Name_____ Date _____

Solve the equation algebraically and graphically.

1. $\frac{1}{4}x + 4 = x - 2$

2. $\frac{1}{2}x + 2 = \frac{7}{8}x + \frac{1}{2}$

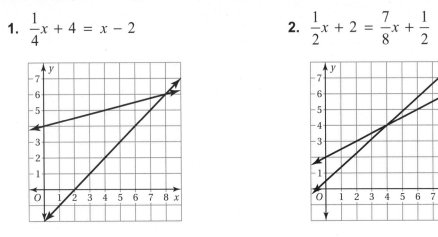

Use a graph to solve the equation. Check your solution.

3. $\frac{1}{2}x + 4 = -x - 11$

4. $-x + 1 = -\frac{1}{4}x - \frac{1}{2}$

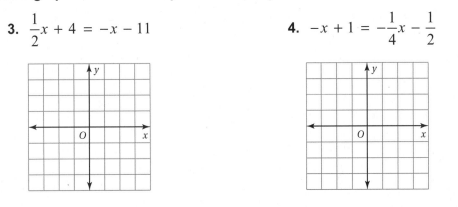

5. On the first day of your garage sale, you earned $12x + 9$ dollars. The next day you earned $22x$ dollars. Is it possible that you earned the same amount each day? Explain.

Name_____ Date_____

 **Fair Game Review**

Evaluate the expression.

1. $\dfrac{6}{7} \cdot \dfrac{2}{3}$

2. $\dfrac{4}{9} \cdot \dfrac{3}{10}$

3. $\dfrac{5}{8} \div \dfrac{5}{6}$

4. $\dfrac{7}{12} \div \dfrac{3}{14}$

5. You have a box of 64 crayons. For an art project, you use $\dfrac{5}{16}$ of the crayons. How many crayons do you use?

6. You make 4 cups of batter for muffins. The recipe calls for $\dfrac{2}{3}$ cup of batter for each muffin. How many muffins does the recipe make?

7. Sales tax is 6.5%. What is the sales tax on an item that costs $22?

8. Your bill at a restaurant is $8.90. What is the amount of a 20% tip on the bill?

9. There are 75 questions on your exam. You answered 96% of the questions correctly. How many questions did you answer correctly?

10. You ask your classmates to name their favorite music genre. Of your 20 classmates, 30% said their favorite music genre is country music. How many students answered country music?

Name_____ Date_____

3.1 Writing Equations in Slope-Intercept Form
For use with Activity 3.1

Essential Question How can you write an equation of a line when you are given the slope and *y*-intercept of the line?

1 ACTIVITY: Writing Equations of Lines

Work with a partner.

$\frac{4}{12}$

- **Find the slope of each line.**
- **Find the *y*-intercept of each line.**
- **Write an equation for each line.**
- **What do the three lines have in common?**

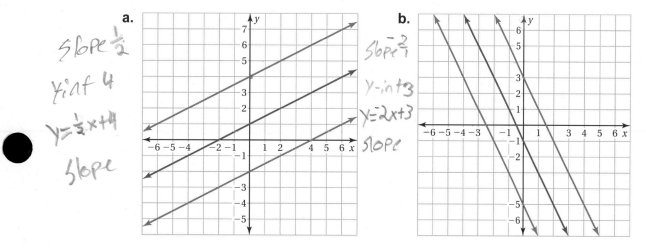

a. slope $\frac{1}{2}$
y-int 4
$y = \frac{1}{2}x + 4$
slope

b. slope $\frac{-2}{1}$
y-int 3
$y = 2x + 3$
slope

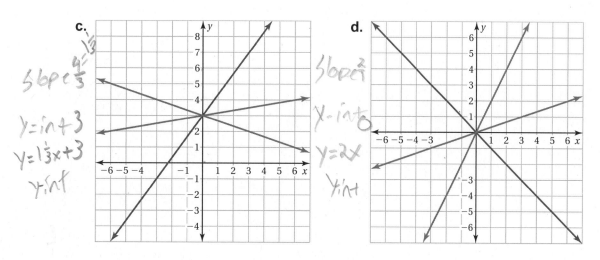

c. slope $\frac{4-1\frac{1}{3}}{3}$
y-int 3
$y = 1\frac{1}{3}x + 3$
y-int

d. slope $\frac{2}{1}$
x-int 0
$y = 2x$
y-int

3.1 Writing Equations in Slope-Intercept Form (continued)

2 **ACTIVITY:** Describing a Parallelogram

Work with a partner.

- Find the area of each parallelogram.

- Write an equation for each side of each parallelogram.

- What do you notice about the slopes of the opposite sides of each parallelogram?

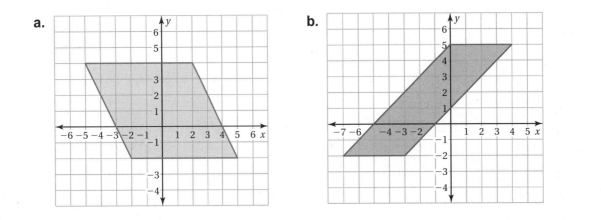

a.

b.

3 **ACTIVITY:** Interpreting the Slope and *y*-Intercept

Work with a partner. The graph shows a trip taken by a car where *t* is the time (in hours) and *y* is the distance (in miles) from Phoenix.

a. How far from Phoenix was the car at the beginning of the trip?

300miles

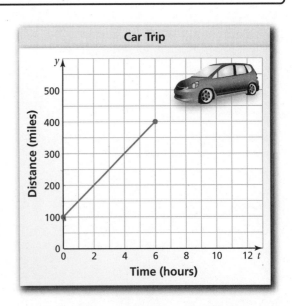

Car Trip

3.1 **Writing Equations in Slope-Intercept Form** (continued)

    b. What was the car's speed?

    c. How long did the trip last?

    d. How far from Phoenix was the car at the end of the trip?

What Is Your Answer?

    4. IN YOUR OWN WORDS How can you write an equation of a line when you are given the slope and y-intercept of the line? Give an example that is different from those in Activities 1, 2, and 3.

Name _____ Date _____

Write an equation of the line in slope-intercept form.

1.
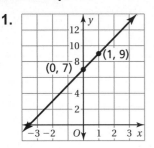

2.
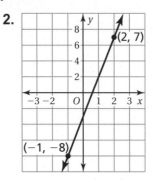

3.
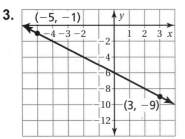

4.
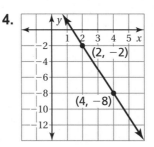

Just slope

Write an equation of the line that passes through the points.

5. $(3, 8), (-2, 8)$

6. $(4, 3), (6, -3)$

7. $(-1, 0), (-5, 0)$

8. You organize a garage sale. You have $30 at the beginning of the sale. You earn an average of $20 per hour. Write an equation that represents the amount of money y you have after x hours.

3.2 **Writing Equations Using a Slope and a Point**
For use with Activity 3.2

Essential Question How can you write an equation of a line when you are given the slope and a point on the line?

1 **ACTIVITY:** Writing Equations of Lines

Work with a partner.

- **Sketch the line that has the given slope and passes through the given point.**
- **Find the *y*-intercept of the line.**
- **Write an equation of the line.**

a. $m = -2$

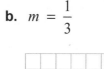

b. $m = \dfrac{1}{3}$

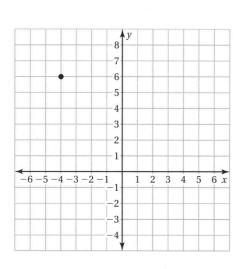

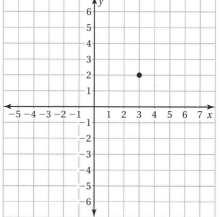

c. $m = -\dfrac{2}{3}$

d. $m = \dfrac{5}{2}$

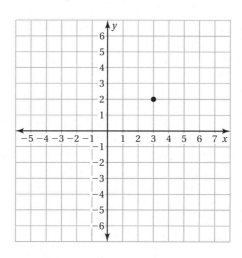

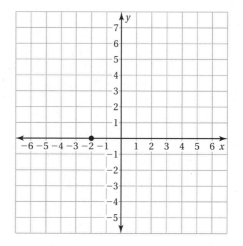

3.2 **Writing Equations Using a Slope and a Point** (continued)

2 **ACTIVITY:** Writing Linear Equations

Work with a partner.

a. For 4 months, you have saved $25 a month. You now have $175 in your savings account.

- Draw a graph that shows the balance in your account after t months.

- Write an equation that represents the balance A after t months.

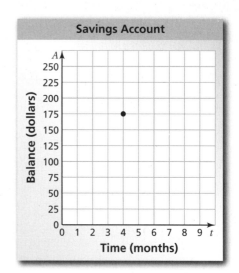

b. For 4 months, you have withdrawn $25 a month from your savings account. Your account balance is now $75.

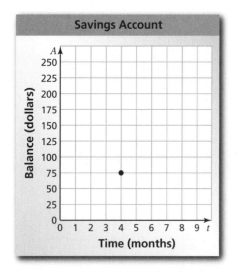

- Draw a graph that shows the balance in your account after t months.

- Write an equation that represents the balance A after t months.

Name_____ Date_____

c. For 6 years, the population of a town has grown by 5000 people per year. The population is now 70,000.

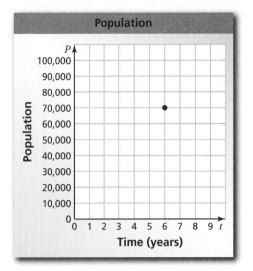

Population

- Draw a graph that shows the population after t years.

- Write an equation that represents the population P after t years.

What Is Your Answer?

3. IN YOUR OWN WORDS How can you write an equation of a line when you are given the slope and a point on the line? Give an example that is different from those in Activities 1 and 2.

Name _____ Date _____

3.2 **Practice**

For use after Lesson 3.2

Write an equation of the line with the given slope that passes through the given point.

1. $m = \dfrac{1}{4}$

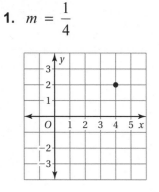

2. $m = -\dfrac{2}{5}$

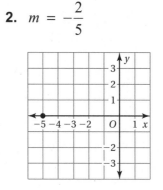

3. $m = -3; (-4, 6)$

4. $m = -\dfrac{4}{3}; (3, -1)$

5. The total cost for bowling includes the fee for shoe rental plus a fee per game. The cost of each game increases the price by $4. After 3 games, the total cost with shoe rental is $14.

    a. Write an equation to represent the total cost y to rent shoes and bowl x games.

    b. How much is shoe rental? How is this represented in the equation?

Name_____ Date _____

Writing Equations Using Two Points
For use with Activity 3.3

Essential Question   How can you write an equation of a line when you are given two points on the line?

1 | **ACTIVITY:** Writing Equations of Lines

Work with a partner.

- **Sketch the line that passes through the given points.**
- **Find the slope and *y*-intercept of the line.**
- **Write an equation of the line.**

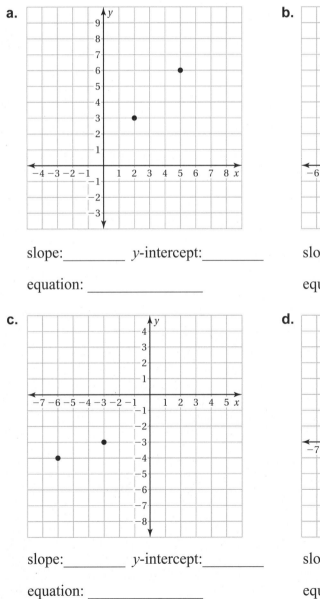

a.

slope:_____ *y*-intercept:_____

equation: _____

b.

slope:_____ *y*-intercept:_____

equation: _____

c.

slope:_____ *y*-intercept:_____

equation: _____

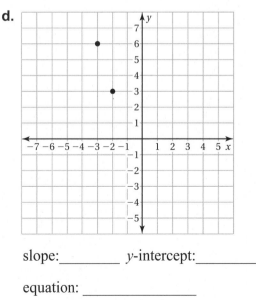

d.

slope:_____ *y*-intercept:_____

equation: _____

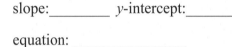

3.3 **Writing Equations Using Two Points** (continued)

2 **ACTIVITY: Writing and Using Linear Equations**

Work with a partner.

a. You are rising in a hot air balloon. After 1 minute, you are 200 feet above the ground. After 4 minutes, you are 800 feet above the ground.

- Write an equation for the height h in terms of the time t.

- Use your equation to find the height of the balloon after 5 minutes.

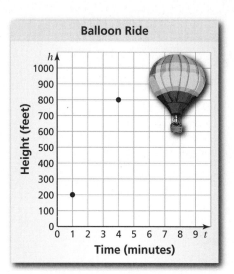

b. After 5 minutes, the hot air balloon starts to descend. After 6 minutes, you are 200 feet above the ground.

- Write an equation for the height h in terms of the time t.

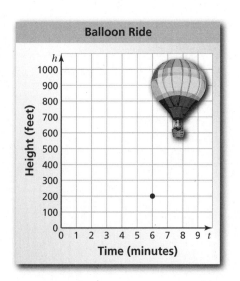

- Use your equation to estimate when the balloon lands on the ground.

Name_____ Date_____

c. You are on a roller coaster. After 3 seconds, you are 190 feet above the ground and have reached maximum speed. One second later, you are 95 feet above the ground.

Roller Coaster Ride

- Write an equation for the height *h* in terms of the time *t*.

- When will you reach ground level?

What Is Your Answer?

3. **IN YOUR OWN WORDS** How can you write an equation of a line when you are given two points on the line? Give an example that is different from those in Activities 1 and 2.

Big Ideas Math Blue 65
Record and Practice Journal

Name _____ Date _____

3.3 Practice
For use after Lesson 3.3

Write an equation of the line that passes through the points.

1.

(graph with points at approximately (1, 7) and (4, 5))

2.

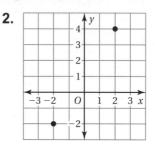

3. $(-3, 0), (-2, 3)$

4. $(-6, 10), (6, -10)$

5. It costs $315 to book a DJ for 3 hours. It costs $525 to book the same DJ for 5 hours. Write an equation that represents the cost y in dollars of booking a DJ for x hours.

6. Water comes out of a garden hose at a constant rate to fill a pool. After 3 minutes, the pool is filled with 30 gallons of water. After 6.5 minutes, the pool is filled with 65 gallons of water.

   a. Write an equation that represents the number of gallons of water y in the pool after x minutes.

   b. How long will it take to fill a pool that needs 10,000 gallons of water?

3.4 Solving Real-Life Problems
For use with Activity 3.4

Essential Question How can you use a linear equation in two variables to model and solve a real-life problem?

> **1** **EXAMPLE:** Writing a Story

Write a story that uses the graph at the right.

- **In your story, interpret the slope of the line, the *y*-intercept, and the *x*-intercept.**

- **Make a table that shows data from the graph.**

- **Label the axes of the graph with units.**

- **Draw pictures for your story.**

There are many possible stories. Here is one about a reef tank.

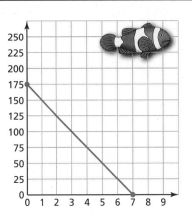

Tom works at an aquarium shop on Saturdays. One Saturday, when Tom gets to work, he is asked to clean a 175-gallon reef tank.

His first job is to drain the tank. He puts a hose into the tank and starts a siphon. Tom wonders if the tank will finish draining before he leaves work.

He measures the amount of water that is draining out and finds that 12.5 gallons drain out in 30 minutes. So, he figures that the rate is 25 gallons per hour. To see when the tank will be empty, Tom makes a table and draws a graph.

x-intercept: number of hours to empty the tank

x	0	1	2	3	4	5	6	7
y	175	150	125	100	75	50	25	0

y-intercept: amount of water in full tank

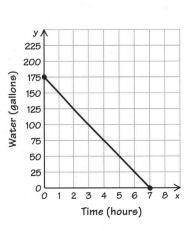

From the table and also from the graph, Tom sees that the tank will be empty after 7 hours. This will give him 1 hour to wash the tank before going home.

3.4 **Solving Real-Life Problems** (continued)

2 **ACTIVITY:** Writing a Story

Work with a partner. Write a story that uses the graph of a line.

- **In your story, interpret the slope of the line, the *y*-intercept, and the *x*-intercept.**

- **Make a table that shows data from the graph.**

- **Label the axes of the graph with units.**

- **Draw pictures for your story.**

Name_____ Date_____

3 **ACTIVITY:** Drawing Graphs

Work with a partner. Describe a real-life problem that has the given rate and intercepts. Draw a line that represents the problem.

a. Rate: −30 feet per second
 y-intercept: 150 feet
 x-intercept: 5 seconds

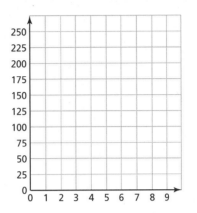

b. Rate: −25 dollars per month
 y-intercept: $200
 x-intercept: 8 months

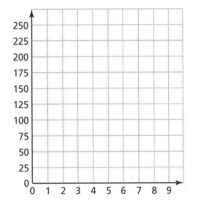

What Is Your Answer?

4. IN YOUR OWN WORDS How can you use a linear equation in two variables to model and solve a real-life problem? List three different rates that can be represented by slopes in real-life problems.

3.4 **Practice**
For use after Lesson 3.4

Describe a real-life problem that has the given rate and intercepts. Draw a line that represents the problem.

1. Rate: −6 feet per year
   y-intercept: 24 feet
   x-intercept: 4 years

2. Rate: −2 pages per minute
   y-intercept: 280 pages
   x-intercept: 140 minutes

3. You are buying shirts for an organization. You have $120 to spend. The number of short-sleeved shirts y you buy after buying x long-sleeved shirts is $y = -1.2x + 24$.

   a. Graph the equation.

   b. Interpret the x- and y-intercepts.

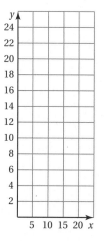

4. The graph relates the percent of battery life y left in an MP3 player to the amount of playing time it has left. Write an equation of the line.

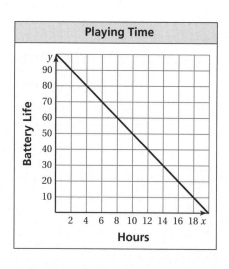

3.5 Writing Systems of Linear Equations
For use with Activity 3.5

Essential Question How can you use a system of linear equations to model and solve a real-life problem?

---

1 ACTIVITY: Writing a System

Work with a partner.

- **Peak Valley Middle School has 1200 students. Its enrollment is decreasing by 30 students per year.**

- **Southern Tier Middle School has 500 students. Its enrollment is increasing by 40 students per year.**

- **In how many years will the two schools have equal enrollments?**

a. USE A TABLE Use a table to answer the question.

Now

Year, x	0	1	2	3	4	5	6	7	8	9	10
Peak Valley MS, P	1200										
Southern Tier MS, S	500										

b. USE A GRAPH Write a linear equation that represents each enrollment.

$P = $ _____

$S = $ _____

Then graph each equation and find the point of intersection to answer the question.

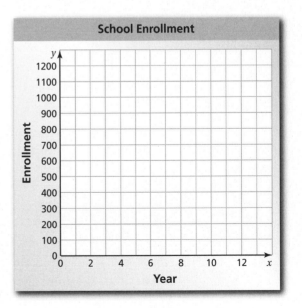

Name_____ Date _____

3.5 **Writing Systems of Linear Equations** (continued)

c. USE ALGEBRA Answer the question by setting the expressions for *P* and *S* equal to each other and solving for *x*.

2 **ACTIVITY:** Writing a System

Work with a partner. The table shows the enrollments of Sizemore Middle School and Wright Middle School for 7 years.

Year, *x*	0	1	2	3	4	5	6
Sizemore MS, *S*	1500	1438	1423	1350	1308	1247	1204
Wright MS, *W*	825	854	872	903	927	946	981

From the enrollment pattern, do you think the two schools will ever have the same enrollment? If so, when?

a. Plot the enrollments of each middle school.

b. Draw a line that approximately fits the points for each middle school.

c. Estimate the year in which the schools will have the same enrollment.

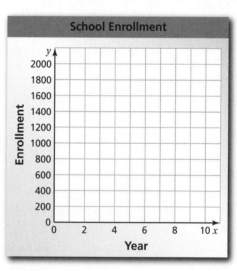

d. Write an equation for each line.

    S = _____

    W = _____

3.5 **Writing Systems of Linear Equations** (continued)

e. USE ALGEBRA Answer the question by setting the expressions for S and W equal to each other and solving for x.

What Is Your Answer?

3. **IN YOUR OWN WORDS** How can you use a system of linear equations to model and solve a real-life problem?

4. **PROJECT** Use the Internet, a newspaper, a magazine, or some other reference to find two sets of real-life data that can be modeled by linear equations.

   a. List the data in a table.

   b. Graph the data. Find a line to represent each data set.

   c. If possible, estimate when the two quantities will be equal.

Name _____ Date _____

Practice
For use after Lesson 3.5

Write a system of linear equations to represent the situation. Then, answer the question using (a) a table, (b) a graph, and (c) algebra.

1. The cost of buying pans and making pies for a bake sale is $15 plus $3.50 for each pie. The revenue is $5.00 for each pie. After how many pies x will the cost equal the revenue?

Cost:	Buying pans and ingredients	is	$15	plus $3.50 times	number of pies.

Revenue:	Income from selling pies	is	$5	times	number of pies.

2. You buy 16 candles. Large candles cost $7 each and small candles cost $3 each. You spend $76. How many large candles x and small candles y did you buy?

Number of candles:	Number of large candles	plus	number of small candles	is	16.

Cost of candles:	$7 times	number of large candles	plus $3 times	number of small candles	is	$76.

3. There are 62 time slots for cheerleading tryouts on Saturday and Sunday. There are 14 more slots on Saturday than on Sunday. Find the number of Saturday time slots x and the number of Sunday time slots y.

Name_____ Date_____

Describe the pattern of inputs *x* and outputs *y*.

1. Input, *x* Output, *y*

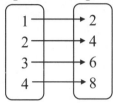

1	2
2	4
3	6
4	8

2. Input, *x* Output, *y*

−2	0
0	5
2	10
4	15

3.

Input, *x*	−3	1	5	9	13
Output, *y*	−4	−1	2	5	8

4.

Input, *x*	−2	−1	0	1	2
Output, *y*	2	−5	−12	−19	−26

5. The table shows the number of customers *y* in *x* hours. Describe the inputs and outputs.

Hours, *x*	0	1	2	3	4
Customers, *y*	0	15	30	45	60

Chapter 4

Fair Game Review (continued)

Draw a mapping diagram for the graph. Then describe the pattern of inputs and outputs.

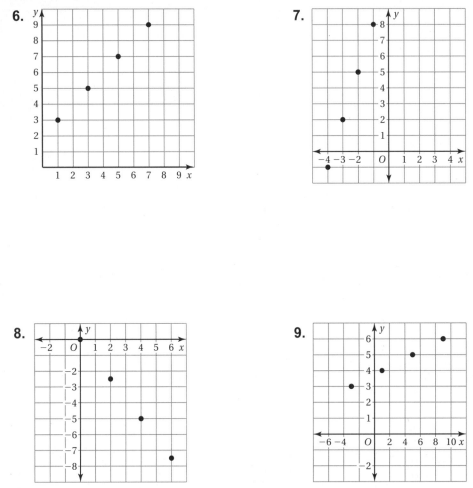

6.

7.

8.

9.

10. In basketball, for each shot you make from inside the three-point circle, you score two points. Draw a mapping diagram for inputs 0, 2, 4, 6, and 8.

4.1 Domain and Range of a Function
For use with Activity 4.1

Essential Question   How can you find the domain and range of a function?

> **1   ACTIVITY:** The Domain and Range of a Function

Work with a partner. The table shows the number of adult and child tickets sold for a school concert.

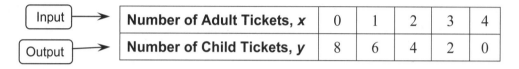

Input →	**Number of Adult Tickets, x**	0	1	2	3	4
Output →	**Number of Child Tickets, y**	8	6	4	2	0

The variables x and y are related by the linear equation $4x + 2y = 16$.

a. Write the equation in **function form** by solving for y.

b. The **domain** of a function is the set of all input values. Find the domain of the function represented by the table.

   Domain = _____

   Why is $x = 5$ not in the domain of the function?

   Why is $x = \dfrac{1}{2}$ not in the domain of the function?

c. The **range** of a function is the set of all output values. Find the range of the function represented by the table.

   Range = _____

Name _____   Date _____

4.1   **Domain and Range of a Function** (continued)

d. Functions can be described in many ways.

- by an equation

- by an input-output table

- in words

- by a graph

- as a set of ordered pairs

Use the graph to write the function as a set of ordered pairs.

---

2   **ACTIVITY:** Finding Domains and Ranges

Work with a partner.

- **Complete each input-output table.**

- **Find the domain and range of each function represented by the table.**

a. $y = -3x + 4$

x	−2	−1	0	1	2
y					

b. $y = \frac{1}{2}x - 6$

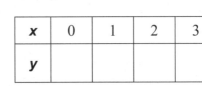

x	0	1	2	3	4
y					

c.

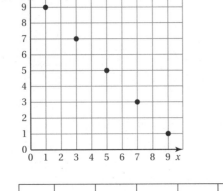

x					
y					

d.

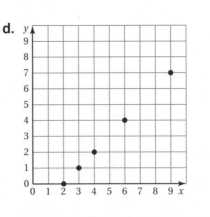

x					
y					

---

78   **Big Ideas Math Blue**
Record and Practice Journal

4.1 **Domain and Range of a Function** (continued)

What Is Your Answer?

3. **IN YOUR OWN WORDS** How can you find the domain and range of a function?

4. **The following are general rules for finding a person's foot length.**

To find the length y (in inches) of a woman's foot, divide her shoe size x by 3 and add 7.

To find the length y (in inches) of a man's foot, divide his shoe size x by 3 and add 7.3.

a. Write an equation for one of the statements.

b. Make an input-output table for the function in part (a). Use shoe sizes $5\frac{1}{2}$ to 12.

c. Label the domain and range of the function represented by the table.

Name _____ Date _____

Find the domain and range of the function represented by the graph.

1.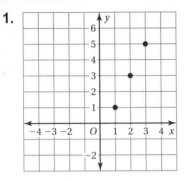

2.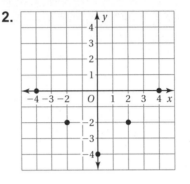

Complete the input-output table for the function. Then find the domain and range of the function represented by the table.

3. $y = 2x - 5$

x	−2	−1	0	1
y				

4. $y = -\dfrac{1}{2}x + 3$

x	0	2	4	6
y				

5. A factory that makes frozen pies produces 300 pies per minute.

   a. Write an equation in function form that represents the number y of pies made each hour x.

   b. Create an input-output table for the equation in part (a). Use inputs 1, 2, 4, 8, and 10.

   c. Find the domain and range of the function represented by the table.

Name_____ Date_____

 4.2 **Discrete and Continuous Domains**
For use with Activity 4.2

Essential Question How can you decide whether the domain of a function is discrete or continuous?

┌───┐
1 **EXAMPLE:** Discrete and Continuous Domains
└───┘

In Activities 1 and 2 in Section 2.4, you studied two real-life problems represented by the same equation.

$$4x + 2y = 16 \text{ or } y = -2x + 8$$

a.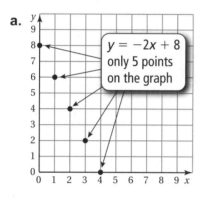

$y = -2x + 8$
only 5 points on the graph

Domain (*x*-values): 0, 1, 2, 3, 4
Range (*y*-values): 8, 6, 4, 2, 0
The domain is **discrete** because it consists of only the numbers 0, 1, 2, 3, and 4.

b.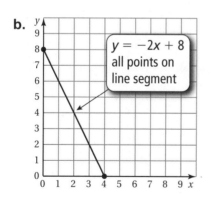

$y = -2x + 8$
all points on line segment

Domain (*x*-values): $x \geq 0$ and $x \leq 4$
(All numbers from 0 to 4)
Range (*y*-values): $y \geq 0$ and $y \leq 8$
(All numbers from 0 to 8)
The domain is **continuous** because it consists of all numbers from 0 and 4 on the number line.

Big Ideas Math Blue **81**
Record and Practice Journal

Name _____ Date _____

2 **ACTIVITY:** Discrete and Continuous Domains

Work with a partner.

- **Write a function to represent each problem.**

- **Graph each function.**

- **Describe the domain and range of each function. Is the domain discrete or continuous?**

a. You are in charge of reserving hotel rooms for a youth soccer team. Each room costs $69, plus $6 tax, per night. You need each room for two nights. You need 10 to 16 rooms. Write a function for the total hotel cost.

b. The airline you are using for the soccer trip needs an estimate of the total weight of the team's luggage. You determine that there will be 36 pieces of luggage and each piece will weigh from 25 to 45 pounds. Write a function for the total weight of the luggage.

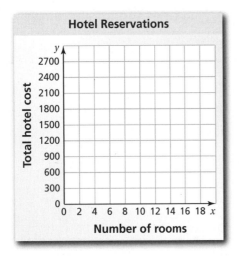

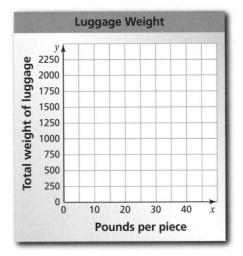

4.2 Discrete and Continuous Domains (continued)

What Is Your Answer?

3. **IN YOUR OWN WORDS** How can you decide whether the domain of a function is discrete or continuous? Describe two real-life examples of functions: one with a discrete domain and one with a continuous domain.

Name _____ Date _____

Graph the function. Is the domain discrete or continuous?

1.

Input Length, x (inches)	Output Area, y (square inches)
2	12
4	24
6	36

2.

Input Shirts, x	Output Cost, y (dollars)
0	0
1	9.25
2	18.50

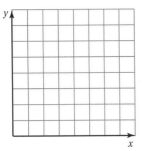

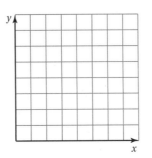

3. The function $c = 20 + 10m$ represents the amount of calories you burn after m minutes of exercising. Graph the function using a domain of 0, 5, 10, and 15. Is the domain discrete or continuous?

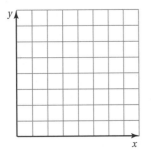

4. You buy cards to send to family and friends for their birthdays. The function $y = 2.5x$ represents the cost y of the number of cards x you buy.

   a. Is 8 in the domain? Explain.

   b. Is 40 in the range? Explain.

Name_____ Date_____

4.3 Linear Function Patterns
For use with Activity 4.3

Essential Question   How can you use a linear function to describe a linear pattern?

1 ACTIVITY: Finding Linear Patterns

Work with a partner.

- Plot the points from the table in a coordinate plane.

- Write a linear equation for the function.

a.

x	0	2	4	6	8
y	150	125	100	75	50

b.

x	4	6	8	10	12
y	15	20	25	30	35

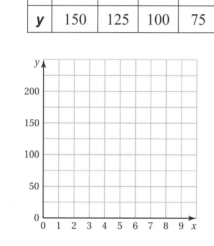

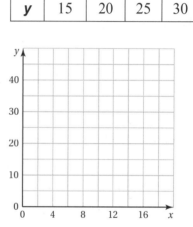

c.

x	−4	−2	0	2	4
y	4	6	8	10	12

d.

x	−4	−2	0	2	4
y	1	0	−1	−2	−3

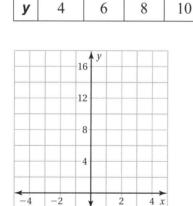

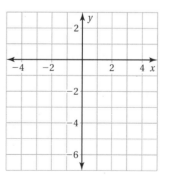

4.3 **Linear Function Patterns** (continued)

2 **ACTIVITY:** Finding Linear Patterns

Work with a partner. The table shows a familiar linear pattern from geometry.

- **Write a linear function that relates _y_ to _x_.**

- **What do the variables _x_ and _y_ represent?**

- **Graph the linear function.**

a.

x	1	2	3	4	5
y	2π	4π	6π	8π	10π

b.

x	1	2	3	4	5
y	10	12	14	16	18

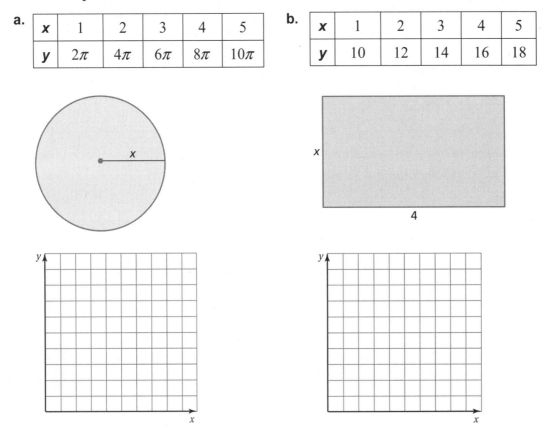

Name_____ Date_____

4.3 **Linear Function Patterns** (continued)

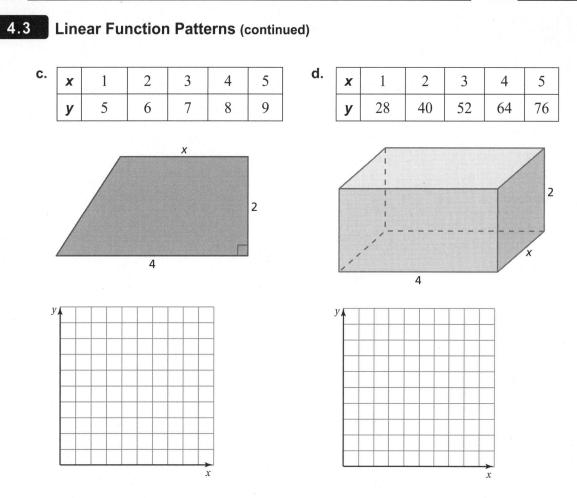

c.

x	1	2	3	4	5
y	5	6	7	8	9

d.

x	1	2	3	4	5
y	28	40	52	64	76

What Is Your Answer?

3. **IN YOUR OWN WORDS** How can you use a linear function to describe a linear pattern?

4. Describe the strategy you used to find the linear functions in Activities 1 and 2.

Name _____ Date _____

 Practice
For use after Lesson 4.3

Use the graph or the table to write a linear function that relates _y_ to _x_.

1.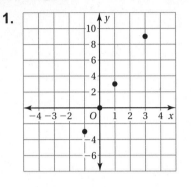

2.

3.

x	0	1	2	3
y	5	7	9	11

4.

x	−2	0	2	4
y	−1	−2	−3	−4

5. The table shows the distance traveled _y_ (in miles) after _x_ hours.

x	0	2	4	6
y	0	120	240	360

  a. Graph the data. Is the domain discrete or continuous?

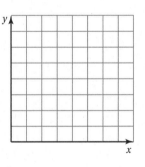

  b. Write a linear function that relates _y_ to _x_.

  c. What is the distance traveled after three hours?

88 **Big Ideas Math Blue**
Record and Practice Journal

Name_____ Date_____

4.4 Comparing Linear and Nonlinear Functions
For use with Activity 4.4

Essential Question How can you recognize when a pattern in real life is linear or nonlinear?

1 ACTIVITY: Finding Patterns for Similar Figures

Work with a partner. Complete each table for the sequence of similar rectangles. Graph the data in each table. Decide whether each pattern is linear or nonlinear.

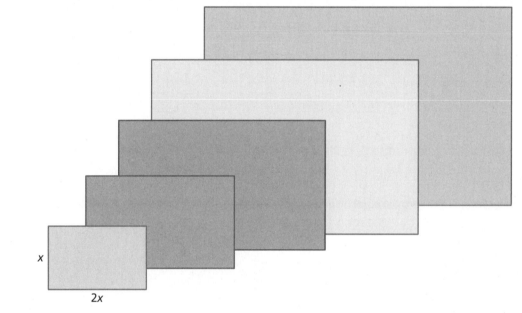

a. Perimeters of Similar Rectangles

x	1	2	3	4	5
P					

b. Areas of Similar Rectangles

x	1	2	3	4	5
A					

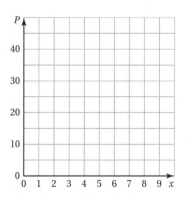

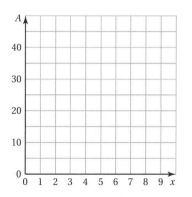

4.4 **Comparing Linear and Nonlinear Functions** (continued)

2 **ACTIVITY:** Comparing Linear and Nonlinear Functions

Work with a partner. The table shows the height *h* (in feet) of a falling object at *t* seconds.

- **Graph the data in the table.**

- **Decide whether the graph is linear or nonlinear.**

- **Compare the two falling objects. Which one has an increasing speed?**

a. Falling parachute jumper

t	0	1	2	3	4
h	300	285	270	255	240

b. Falling bowling ball

t	0	1	2	3	4
h	300	284	236	156	44

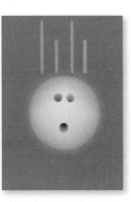

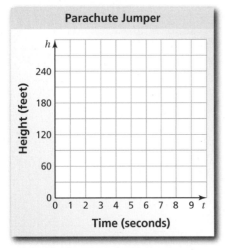

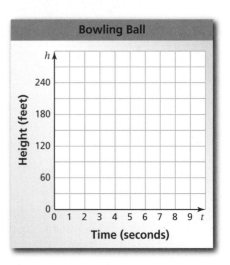

4.4 **Comparing Linear and Nonlinear Functions** (continued)

What Is Your Answer?

3. **IN YOUR OWN WORDS** How can you recognize when a pattern in real life is linear or nonlinear? Describe two real-life patterns: one that is linear and one that is nonlinear. Use patterns that are different from those described in Activities 1 and 2.

Name _____ Date _____

Graph the data in the table. Decide whether the function is *linear* or *nonlinear*.

1.

x	−2	0	2	4
y	4	0	4	16

2.

x	−1	0	1	2
y	−1	1	3	5

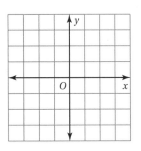

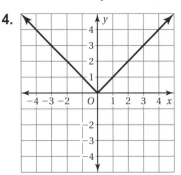

Does the graph represent a *linear* or nonlinear *function*? Explain.

3.

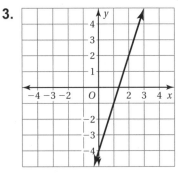

4.

5. The table shows the area of a square with side length *x* inches. Does the table represent a linear or nonlinear function? Explain.

Side Length, x	1	2	3	4
Area, A	1	4	9	16

4.4b **Practice**
For use after Lesson 4.4b

1. The distance y (in miles) traveled by a car in x hours is represented by the equation $y = 70x$. The graph shows the distance traveled by a truck.

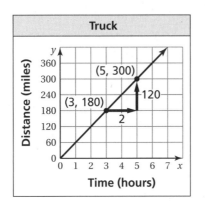

a. Which vehicle is faster?

b. Graph the equation that represents the car in the same coordinate plane as the truck. Compare the steepness of the graphs. What does this mean in the context of the problem?

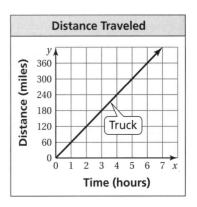

Name _____ Date _____

2. The earnings y (in dollars) of Salesman A working x hours is represented by the function $y = 12.5x + 40$. The table shows the earnings of Salesman B.

	+1	+1	+1	
Time (hours)	1	2	3	4
Earnings (dollars)	20.50	41.00	61.50	82.00

+20.50 +20.50 +20.50

a. Which salesman has a higher hourly wage?

b. Write a function that relates the earnings of Salesman B to the number of hours worked. Graph the functions that represent the earnings of the two salesmen in the same coordinate plane. Interpret the graphs.

Chapter 5 **Fair Game Review**

The polygons are similar. Find the value of x.

1.

2.

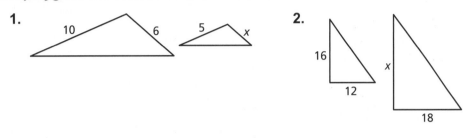

3.

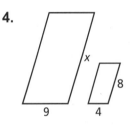

4.

5. The two peaks of a house are similar triangles. What is the value of *x*?

6. The two windows on the house are also similar. What is the value of *x*?

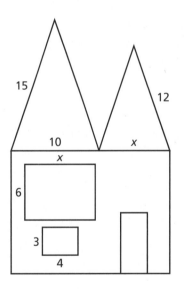

Chapter 5 **Fair Game Review** (continued)

The polygons are similar. Find the value of _x_.

7. The ratio of the perimeters is 2 : 1.

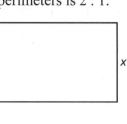

15

_x_

8. The ratio of the perimeters is 2 : 5.

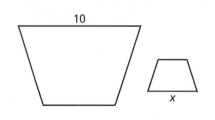

10

_x_

9. The ratio of the perimeters is 4 : 3.

12

_x_

10. The ratio of the perimeters is 3 : 5.

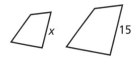

_x_

15

11. Your school builds a new gymnasium that is similar to the old one. The ratio of the perimeters is 2 : 3. The new gymnasium has a length of 90 feet. What was the length of the old gymnasium?

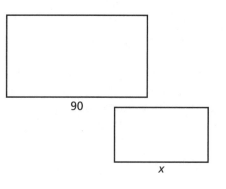

90

_x_

Name_____ Date_____

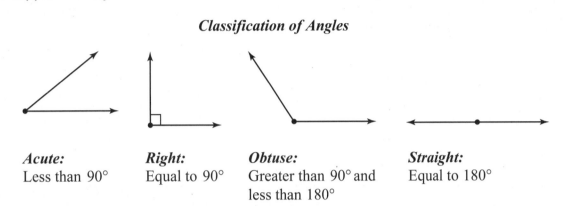

5.1 Classifying Angles
For use with Activity 5.1

Essential Question How can you classify two angles as complementary or supplementary?

Classification of Angles

Acute:
Less than 90°

Right:
Equal to 90°

Obtuse:
Greater than 90° and less than 180°

Straight:
Equal to 180°

① ACTIVITY: Complementary and Supplementary Angles

Work with a partner.

- **Complete each table.**
- **Graph each function. Is the function linear?**
- **Write an equation for *y* as a function of *x*.**
- **Describe the domain of each function.**

a. Two angles are **complementary** if the sum of their measures is 90°. In the table, *x* and *y* are complementary.

x	15°	30°	45°	60°	75°
y					

b. Two angles are **supplementary** if the sum of their measures is 180°. In the table, *x* and *y* are supplementary.

x	30°	60°	90°	120°	150°
y					

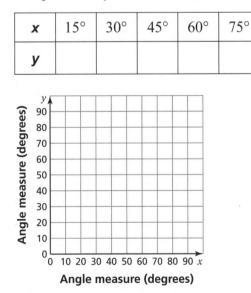

Angle measure (degrees)

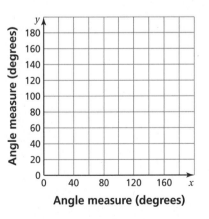

Angle measure (degrees)

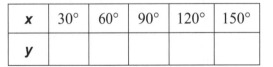

5.1 **Classifying Angles** (continued)

2 **ACTIVITY:** Exploring Rules About Angles

Work with a partner. Complete each sentence with *always*, *sometimes*, **or** *never*.

a. If *x* and *y* are complementary angles, then both *x* and *y* are _____ acute.

b. If *x* and *y* are supplementary angles, then *x* is _____ acute.

c. If *x* is a right angle, then *x* is _____ acute.

3 **ACTIVITY:** Naming Angles

Some angles, such as ∠*A*, **can be named by a single letter. When this does not clearly identify an angle, you should use three letters, as follows.**

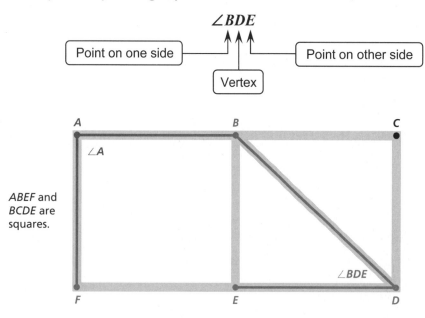

Work with a partner.

a. Name all pairs of complementary angles in the diagram above.

b. Name all pairs of supplementary angles in the diagram above.

5.1 **Classifying Angles** (continued)

What Is Your Answer?

4. **IN YOUR OWN WORDS** How can you classify two angles as complementary or supplementary? Give examples of each type.

5. Find examples of real-life objects that use complementary and supplementary angles. Make a drawing of each object and approximate the degree measure of each angle.

Name _____ Date _____

Tell whether the angles are *complementary*, *supplementary*, or *neither*.

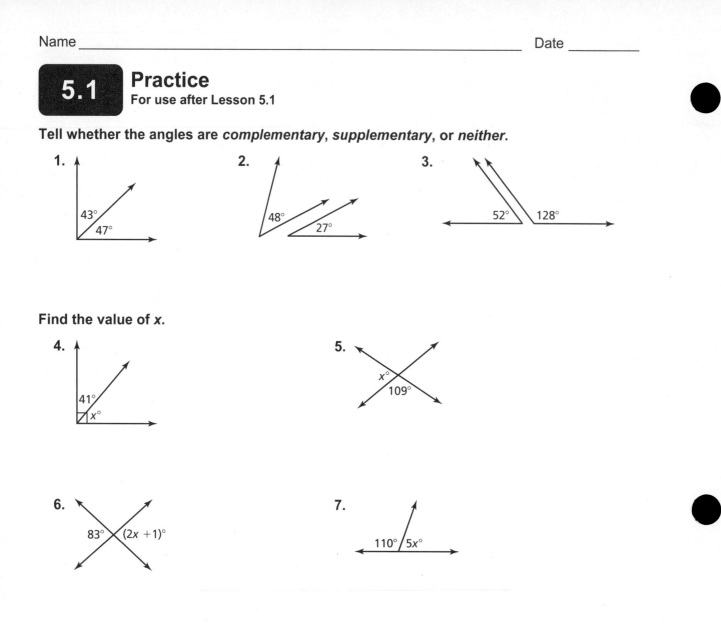

1.

43°
47°

2.

48°
27°

3.

52°   128°

Find the value of *x*.

4.

41°
$x°$

5.

$x°$
109°

6.

83° $(2x + 1)°$

7.

110° / $5x°$

8. Find the value of *x* needed to hit the ball in the hole.

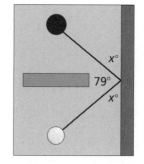

$x°$
79°
$x°$

Name_____ Date_____

5.2 Angles and Sides of Triangles
For use with Activity 5.2

Essential Question How can you classify triangles by their angles?

1 ACTIVITY: Exploring the Angles of a Triangle

Work with a partner.

a. Draw a large triangle that has an obtuse angle on a separate piece of paper. Label the angles *A*, *B*, and *C*.

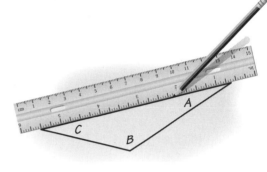

b. Carefully cut out the triangle. Tear off the three corners of the triangle.

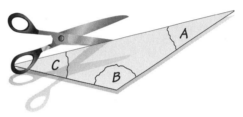

c. Draw a straight line on a piece of paper. Arrange angles *A* and *B* as shown.

d. Place the third angle as shown. What does this tell you about the sum of the measures of the angles?

e. Draw three other triangles that have different shapes. Repeat parts (b)–(d) for each one. Do you get the same results as in part (d)? Explain.

f. Write a rule about the sum of the measures of the angles of a triangle. Compare your rule with the rule you wrote in Activity 2 in Section 1.1. Did you get the same result? Explain.

5.2 **Angles and Sides of Triangles** (continued)

2 **ACTIVITY:** Thinking About Vocabulary

Work with a partner. Talk about the meaning of each name. Use reasoning to define each name. Then match each name with a triangle.

Note: Each triangle has at least one name, but some have more than one name.

a. Right triangle

b. Acute triangle

c. Obtuse triangle

d. Equiangular triangle

e. Equilateral triangle

f. Isosceles triangle

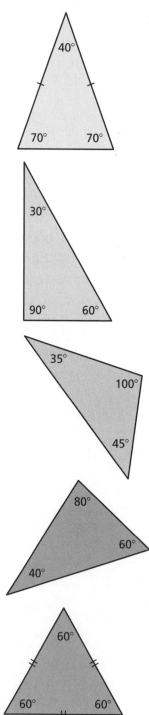

5.2 **Angles and Sides of Triangles** (continued)

3 **ACTIVITY:** Triangles in Art

Work with a partner.

a. Trace four triangles in the painting. Classify each triangle using the names in Activity 2.

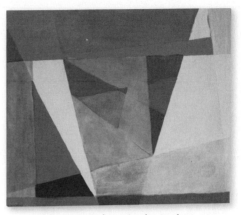

Abstract II by Linda Bahner
www.spiritartist.com

b. Design your own abstract art painting. How many different types of triangles did you use in your painting?

What Is Your Answer?

4. **IN YOUR OWN WORDS** How can you classify triangles by their angles?

5. Find examples of real-life triangles in architecture. Name each type of triangle that you find.

Name _____ Date _____

Practice

For use after Lesson 5.2

Find the value of x. Then classify the triangle in as many ways as possible.

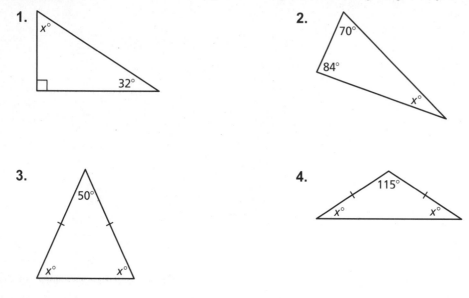

1.

$x°$

$32°$

2.

$70°$

$84°$

$x°$

3.

$50°$

$x°$ $x°$

4.

$115°$

$x°$ $x°$

Tell whether a triangle can have the given angle measures. If not, change the first angle measure so that the angle measures form a triangle.

5. 28°, 42°, 110°   6. 77°, 98°, 15°   7. 31°, 59°, 60°

8. Find the value of x on the clothes hanger. What type of triangle must the hanger be to hang clothes evenly?

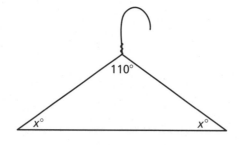

$110°$

$x°$ $x°$

Name_____ Date_____

5.3 Angles of Polygons
For use with Activity 5.3

Essential Question How can you find a formula for the sum of the angle measures of any polygon?

---

1 ACTIVITY: The Sum of the Angle Measures of a Polygon

Work with a partner. Find the sum of the angle measures of each polygon with *n* sides.

a. Sample: Quadrilateral: $n = 4$
Draw a line that divides the quadrilateral into two triangles.

Because the sum of the angle measures of each triangle is 180°, the sum of the angle measures of the quadrilateral is 360°.

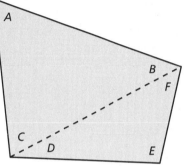

$$(A + B + C) + (D + E + F) = 180° + 180°$$
$$= 360°$$

b. Pentagon: $n = 5$

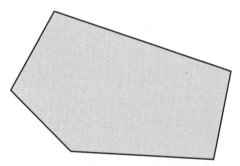

c. Hexagon: $n = 6$

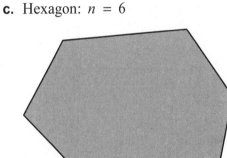

d. Heptagon: $n = 7$

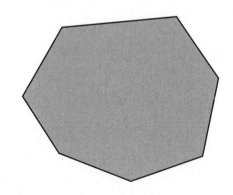

e. Octagon: $n = 8$

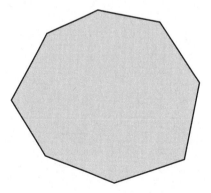

5.3 Angles of Polygons (continued)

2 ACTIVITY: The Sum of the Angle Measures of a Polygon

Work with a partner.

a. Use the table to organize your results from Activity 1.

Sides, n	3	4	5	6	7	8
Angle Sum, S						

b. Plot the points in the table in a coordinate plane.

c. Write a linear equation that relates S to n.

d. What is the domain of the function? Explain your reasoning.

e. Use the function to find the sum of the angle measures of a polygon with 10 sides.

5.3 Angles of Polygons (continued)

3 **ACTIVITY:** The Sum of the Angle Measures of a Polygon

Work with a partner.

A polygon is **convex** if the line segment connecting any two vertices lies entirely inside the polygon. A polygon that is not convex is called **concave**.

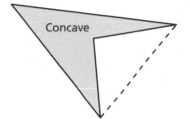

Does the equation you found in Activity 2 apply to concave polygons? Explain.

How can you define the measure of an angle so that your equation applies to *any* polygon?

What Is Your Answer?

4. **IN YOUR OWN WORDS** How can you find a formula for the sum of the angle measures of any polygon?

Name _____ Date _____

Find the sum of the angle measures of the polygon.

1.

2.

3.

Find the value of x.

4.

120°
80°
135°
x°   135°

5.

120°   120°
x°   x°

Find the measure of each angle of the regular polygon.

6.

7.

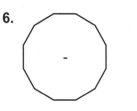

Tell whether the polygon is *convex* or *concave*.

8.

9.

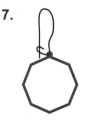

10. In pottery class, you are making a pot that is shaped as a regular hexagon.
What is the measure of each angle in the regular hexagon?

Name_____ Date_____

Essential Question Which properties of triangles make them special among all other types of polygons?

You already know that two triangles are **similar** if and only if the ratios of their corresponding side lengths are equal.

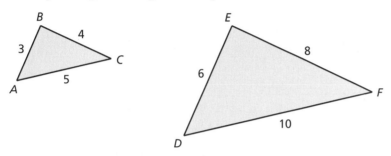

For example, △ABC is similar to △DEF because the ratios of their corresponding side lengths are equal.

$$\frac{6}{3} = \frac{10}{5} = \frac{8}{4}$$

1 ACTIVITY: Angles of Similar Triangles

Work with a partner.

- **Discuss how to make a triangle that is larger than △XYZ and has the *same* angle measures as △XYZ.**

- **Measure the lengths of the sides of the two triangles.**

- **Find the ratios of the corresponding side lengths. Are they all the same? What can you conclude?**

5.4 **Using Similar Triangles** (continued)

2 ACTIVITY: Amazing Triangles

Work with a partner. Use what you know about polygons to decide whether each statement is true. In each case, explain your reasoning.

a.   If two *triangles* are similar, then the ratios of their corresponding side lengths are equal.

  If two *quadrilaterals* are similar, then the ratios of their corresponding side lengths are equal.

b.   If the ratios of the corresponding side lengths of two *triangles* are equal, then the triangles are similar.

  If the ratios of the corresponding side lengths of two *quadrilaterals* are equal, then the quadrilaterals are similar.

c.   If two *triangles* are similar, then their corresponding angles are congruent.

  If two *quadrilaterals* are similar, then their corresponding angles are congruent.

5.4 **Using Similar Triangles** (continued)

d. If the corresponding angles in two *triangles* are congruent, then the triangles are similar.

 If the corresponding angles in two *quadrilaterals* are congruent, then the quadrilaterals are similar.

e. If the corresponding sides of two *triangles* are congruent, then the two triangles have identical shapes.

 If the corresponding sides of two *quadrilaterals* are congruent, then the two quadrilaterals have identical shapes.

What Is Your Answer?

3. **IN YOUR OWN WORDS** Which properties of triangles make them special among all other types of polygons? Describe two careers in which the special properties of triangles are used.

Name _____ Date _____

Tell whether the triangles are similar. Explain.

1.

2.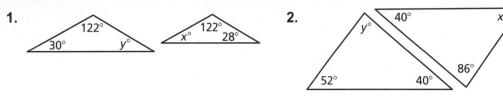

The triangles are similar. Find the value of x.

3.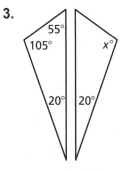

4.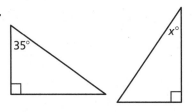

5. You can use similar triangles to find the
height of a tree. Triangle *ABC* is similar
to triangle *DEC*. What is the height of
the tree?

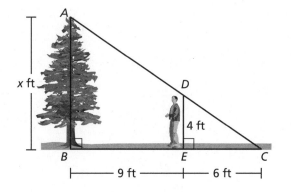

5.5 Parallel Lines and Transversals
For use with Activity 5.5

Essential Question How can you use properties of parallel lines to solve real-life problems?

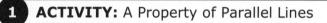

> **1 ACTIVITY:** A Property of Parallel Lines

Work with a partner.

- Talk about what it means for two lines to be parallel. Decide on a strategy for drawing two parallel lines.

- Use your strategy to carefully draw two lines that are parallel in the space below.

- Now, draw a third line that intersects the two parallel lines. This line is called a **transversal**.

- The two parallel lines and the transversal form eight angles. Which of these angles have equal measures? Explain your reasoning.

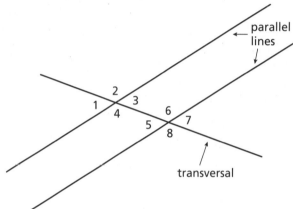

5.5 **Parallel Lines and Transversals** (continued)

2 **ACTIVITY:** Creating Parallel Lines

Work with a partner.

a. If you were building the house in the photograph, how could you make sure that the studs are parallel to each other?

Studs

b. Identify sets of parallel lines and transversals in the photograph.

3 **ACTIVITY:** Indirect Measurement

Work with a partner.

a. Use the fact that two rays from the sun are parallel to explain why $\triangle ABC$ and $\triangle DEF$ are similar.

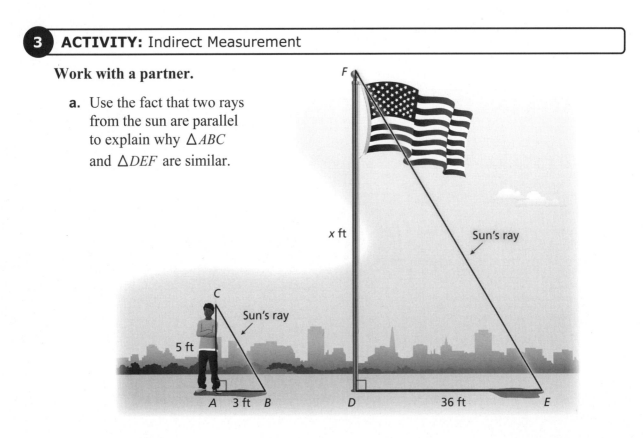

5.5 **Parallel Lines and Transversals** (continued)

b. Explain how to use similar triangles to find the height of the flagpole.

What Is Your Answer?

4. **IN YOUR OWN WORDS** How can you use properties of parallel lines to solve real-life problems? Describe some examples.

5. **INDIRECT MEASUREMENT PROJECT** Work with a partner or in a small group.

a. Explain why the process in Activity 3 is called "indirect" measurement.

b. Use indirect measurement to measure the height of something outside your school (a tree, a building, a flagpole). Before going outside, decide what you need to take with you to do the measurement.

c. Draw a diagram of the indirect measurement process you used. In the diagram, label the lengths that you actually measured and also the lengths that you calculated.

Big Ideas Math Blue **113**
Record and Practice Journal

Name _____ Date _____

Use the figure to find the measures of the numbered angles.

1.

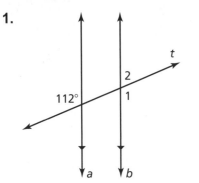

2.

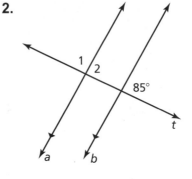

3.

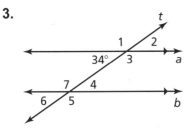

4.

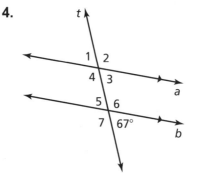

Complete the statement. Explain your reasoning.

5. If the measure of ∠1 = 150°, then the measure of ∠6 = _____.

6. If the measure of ∠3 = 42°, then the measure of ∠5 = _____.

7. If the measure of ∠6 = 28°, then the measure of ∠3 = _____.

8. You paint a border around the top of the walls
    in your room. What angle does x need to be to
    repeat the pattern?

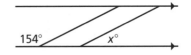

Name____ Date__________

Chapter 6 Fair Game Review

Complete the number sentence with <, >, or =.

1. 3.4 ______ 3.45

2. −6.01 ______ −6.1

3. 3.50 ______ 3.5

4. −0.84 ______ −0.91

Find three decimals that make the number sentence true.

5. $-5.2 \geq$ ______

6. $2.65 >$ ______

7. $-3.18 \leq$ ______

8. $0.03 <$ ______

9. The table shows the times of a 100-meter dash. Order the runners from first place to fifth place.

Runner	Time (seconds)
A	12.60
B	12.55
C	12.49
D	12.63
E	12.495

Chapter 6. **Fair Game Review** (continued)

Evaluate the expression.

10. $10^2 - 48 \div 6 + 25 \cdot 3$

11. $8\left(\dfrac{16}{4}\right) + 2^2 - 11 \cdot 3$

12. $\left(\dfrac{6}{3} + 4\right)^2 \div 4 \cdot 7$

13. $5(9 - 4)^2 - 3^2$

14. $5^2 - 2^2 \cdot 4^2 - 12$

15. $\left(\dfrac{50}{5^2}\right)^2 \div 4$

16. The table shows the numbers of students in 4 classes. The teachers are combining the classes and dividing the students in half to form two groups for a project. Write an expression to represent this situation. How many students are in each group?

Class	Students
1	24
2	32
3	30
4	28

Name_____ Date_____

6.1 Finding Square Roots
For use with Activity 6.1

Essential Question How can you find the side length of a square when you are given the area of the square?

When you multiply a number by itself, you square the number.

Symbol for squaring is 2nd power. → $4^2 = 4 \cdot 4$

$= 16$ 4 squared is 16.

To "undo" this, take the **square root** of the number.

Symbol for square root is a radical sign. → $\sqrt{16} = \sqrt{4^2} = 4$ The square root of 16 is 4.

---

1 ACTIVITY: Finding Square Roots

Work with a partner. Use a square root symbol to write the side length of the square. Then find the square root. Check your answer by multiplying.

a. **Sample:** $s = \sqrt{121} = 11$ **Check:** $11^2 = 11 \cdot 11 = 121$

$$\sqrt{121} = \sqrt{11^2} = 11$$

Area = 121 ft²

s

s

The length of each side of the square is _____11 Ft_____.

b. Area = 81 yd²

s

s

$9^2 = 9 \cdot 9 = 81$
$\sqrt{81} = \sqrt{9^2} = 9$

c. Area = 324 cm²

s

$18^2 = 18 \cdot 18 = 324$
$\sqrt{324} = \sqrt{18^2} = 18$

d. Area = 361 mi²

s

$19^2 = 19 \cdot 19 = 361$
$\sqrt{361} = \sqrt{19^2} = 19$

6.1   Finding Square Roots (continued)

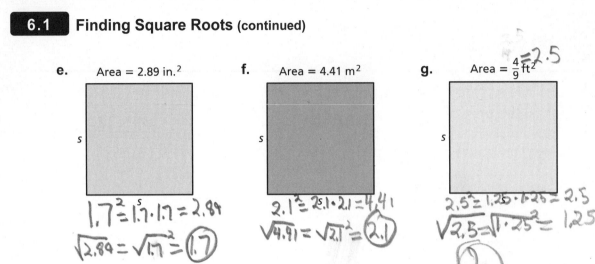

e.   Area = 2.89 in.²

s

$1.7^2 = 1.7 \cdot 1.7 = 2.89$
$\sqrt{2.89} = \sqrt{1.7^2} = \boxed{1.7}$

f.   Area = 4.41 m²

s

$2.1^2 = 2.1 \cdot 2.1 = 4.41$
$\sqrt{4.41} = \sqrt{2.1^2} = \boxed{2.1}$

g.   Area = $\frac{4}{9}$ ft²   = 2.5

s

$2.5^2 = 1.25 \cdot 1.25 = 2.5$
$\sqrt{2.5} = \sqrt{1.25^2} = 1.25$

$\boxed{\frac{2}{3}}$

---

2 ACTIVITY: The Period of a Pendulum

Work with a partner.

The period of a pendulum is the time (in seconds) it takes the pendulum to swing back *and* forth.

The period _T_ is represented by $T = 1.1\sqrt{L}$, where _L_ is the length of the pendulum (in feet).

Complete the table. Then graph the function on the next page. Is the function linear?

L

L	1.00	1.96	3.24	4.00	4.84	6.25	7.29	7.84	9.00
T	1.1	1.54	1.88	2.0	2.2	2.5	2.7	2.8	3.0
			1.98	2.2	2.42	2.75	2.97	3.08	3.3

6.1 **Finding Square Roots** (continued)

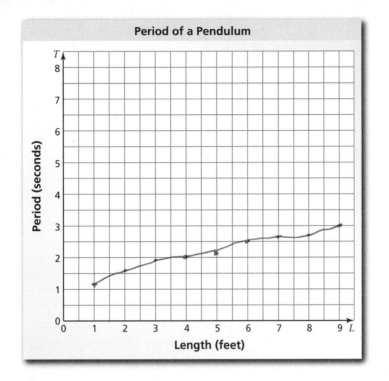

Period of a Pendulum

Period (seconds) — vertical axis (0 to 8)

Length (feet) — horizontal axis (0 to 9, L)

What Is Your Answer?

3. **IN YOUR OWN WORDS** How can you find the side length of a square when you are given the area of a square? Give an example. How can you check your answer? What multiplied by itself gets the area

$121 Ft^2$ Area

$11 \times 11 = 121 Ft^2$

Name _____ Date _____

6.1 Practice
For use after Lesson 6.1

Find the two square roots of the number.

1. 16

2. 100

3. 196

Find the square root(s).

4. $\sqrt{169}$

5. $\sqrt{\dfrac{4}{225}}$

6. $-\sqrt{12.25}$

Evaluate the expression.

7. $2\sqrt{36} + 9$

8. $8 - 11\sqrt{\dfrac{25}{121}}$

9. $3\left(\sqrt{\dfrac{125}{5}} - 8\right)$

10. A trampoline has an area of 49π square feet. What is the diameter of the trampoline?

11. The volume of a cylinder is 75π cubic inches. The cylinder has a height of 3 inches. What is the radius of the base of the cylinder?

6.2 The Pythagorean Theorem
For use with Activity 6.2

Essential Question How are the lengths of the sides of a right triangle related?

Pythagoras was a Greek mathematician and philosopher who discovered one of the most famous rules in mathematics. In mathematics, a rule is called a **theorem**. So, the rule that Pythagoras discovered is called the Pythagorean Theorem.

Pythagoras
(c. 570 B.C.–c. 490 B.C.)

1 ACTIVITY: Discovering the Pythagorean Theorem

Work with a partner.

a. On grid paper, draw any right triangle. Label the lengths of the two shorter sides (the **legs**) a and b.

b. Label the length of the longest side (the **hypotenuse**) c.

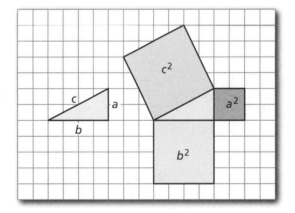

c. Draw squares along each of the three sides. Label the areas of the three squares a^2, b^2, and c^2.

d. Cut out the three squares. Make eight copies of the right triangle and cut them out. Arrange the figures to form two identical larger squares.

e. What does this tell you about the relationship among a^2, b^2, and c^2?

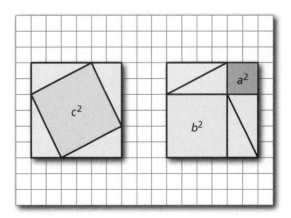

Name _____ Date _____

2 **ACTIVITY:** Finding the Length of the Hypotenuse

Work with a partner. Use the result of Activity 1 to find the length of the hypotenuse of each right triangle.

a.

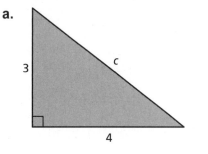

b.

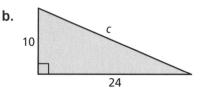

c.

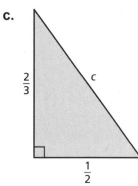

d.

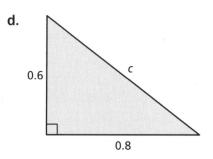

Name_____ Date _____

3 **ACTIVITY:** Finding the Length of a Leg

Work with a partner. Use the result of Activity 1 to find the length of the leg of each right triangle.

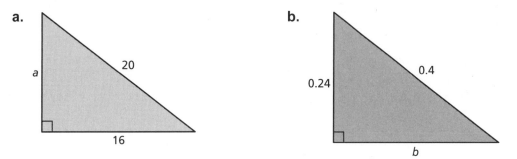

a.

b.

What Is Your Answer?

4. **IN YOUR OWN WORDS** How are the lengths of the sides of a right triangle related? Give an example using whole numbers.

Big Ideas Math Blue **123**
Record and Practice Journal

6.2 Practice
For use after Lesson 6.2

Find the missing length of the triangle.

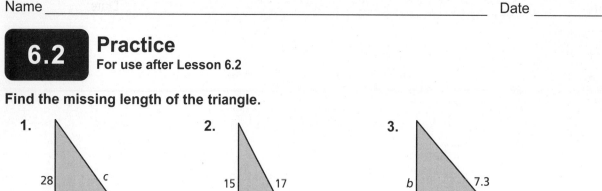

1.
28, c, 21

2.
15, 17, a

3.
b, 7.3, 4.8

Find the value of _x_.

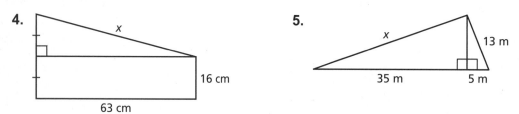

4.
x, 16 cm, 63 cm

5.
x, 13 m, 35 m, 5 m

6. In wood shop, you make a bookend that is in the shape of a right triangle. What is the base _b_ of the bookend?

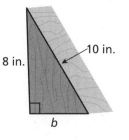

8 in., 10 in., b

6.3 Approximating Square Roots
For use with Activity 6.3

Essential Question How can you find decimal approximations of square roots that are irrational?

You already know that a rational number is a number that can be written as the ratio of two integers. Numbers that cannot be written as the ratio of two integers are called **irrational**.

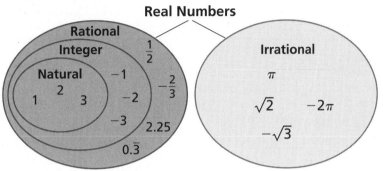

Real Numbers

Rational
Integer
Natural
1 2 3
−1
−2
−3
$\frac{1}{2}$
$-\frac{2}{3}$
2.25
$0.\overline{3}$

Irrational
π
$\sqrt{2}$ -2π
$-\sqrt{3}$

---

1 ACTIVITY: Approximating Square Roots

Work with a partner.

Archimedes was a Greek mathematician, physicist, engineer, inventor, and astronomer.

a. Archimedes tried to find a rational number whose square is 3. Here are two that he tried.

$$\frac{265}{153} \text{ and } \frac{1351}{780}$$

Are either of these numbers equal to $\sqrt{3}$? How can you tell?

b. Use a calculator with a square root key to approximate $\sqrt{3}$.

Write the number on a piece of paper. Then enter it into the calculator and square it. Then subtract 3. Do you get 0? Explain.

6.3   Approximating Square Roots (continued)

   c. Calculators did not exist in the time of Archimedes. How do you think he might have approximated $\sqrt{3}$?

2   ACTIVITY: Approximating Square Roots Geometrically

Work with a partner.

   a. Use grid paper and the given scale to draw a horizontal line segment 1 unit in length. Draw your segment near the bottom of the grid. Label this segment AC.

   b. Draw a vertical line segment 2 units in length. Draw your segment near the left edge of the grid. Label this segment DC.

   c. Set the point of a compass on A. Set the compass to 2 units. Swing the compass to intersect segment DC. Label this intersection as B.

   d. Use the Pythagorean Theorem to show that the length of segment BC is $\sqrt{3}$ units.

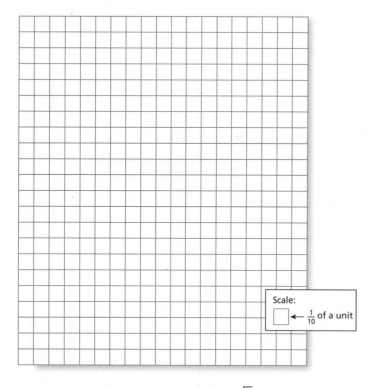

Scale:

☐ ← $\frac{1}{10}$ of a unit

   e. Use the grid paper to approximate $\sqrt{3}$.

Name_____ Date _____

What Is Your Answer?

3. Repeat Activity 2 for a triangle in which segment *CA* is 2 units and segment *BA* is 3 units. Use the Pythagorean Theorem to show that segment *BC* is $\sqrt{5}$ units. Use the grid paper to approximate $\sqrt{5}$.

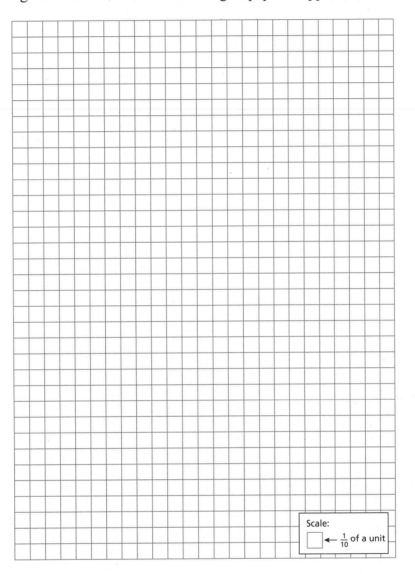

Scale:

□ ← $\frac{1}{10}$ of a unit

4. **IN YOUR OWN WORDS** How can you find decimal approximations of square roots that are irrational?

Name _____ Date _____

Practice
For use after Lesson 6.3

Tell whether the number is *rational* or *irrational*. Explain.

1. $\sqrt{12}$

2. $-\dfrac{3}{7}$

3. $0.4\overline{89}$

Estimate to the nearest integer.

4. $\sqrt{8}$

5. $\sqrt{60}$

6. $-\sqrt{\dfrac{172}{25}}$

Which number is greater? Explain.

7. $\sqrt{88},\ 12$

8. $-\sqrt{18},\ -6$

9. $14.5,\ \sqrt{220}$

10. The velocity in meters per second of a ball that is dropped from a window at a height of 10.5 meters is represented by the equation $v = \sqrt{2(9.8)(10.5)}$. Estimate the velocity of the ball. Round your answer to the nearest tenth.

11. The area of a square table cloth is 30 square feet. Estimate the length of one side of the tablecloth. Round your answer to the nearest tenth.

Name_____ Date_____

Find the cube root of the number.

   1. -64 **2.** 27 **3.** -216

   4. 512 **5.** $\dfrac{1}{125}$ **6.** -0.064

Find the surface area of the cube.

   7. Volume $= 8 \text{ m}^3$ **8.** Volume $= 343 \text{ cm}^3$

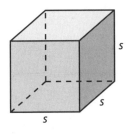   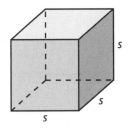

   9. Volume $= 27 \text{ in.}^3$ **10.** Volume $= 1000 \text{ ft}^3$

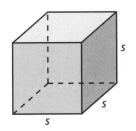   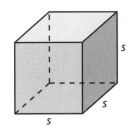

6.3b **Practice** (continued)

Estimate the square root to the nearest tenth.

11. $\sqrt{66}$

12. $-\sqrt{7}$

13. $-\sqrt{34}$

14. $\sqrt{90}$

Complete the statement with < or >.

15. $\sqrt{12}$ _____ $-\sqrt{17}$

16. π _____ $\sqrt{10}$

17. $\sqrt[3]{260}$ _____ $\sqrt{41}$

18. $\sqrt[3]{-95}$ _____ $-\sqrt{22}$

Name_____ Date _____

6.4 Simplifying Square Roots
For use with Activity 6.4

Essential Question How can you use a square root to describe the golden ratio?

Two quantities are in the *golden ratio* if the ratio between the sum of the quantities and the greater quantity is the same as the ratio between the greater quantity and the lesser quantity.

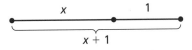

$$\frac{x+1}{x} = \frac{x}{1}$$

In a future algebra course, you will be able to prove that the golden ratio is

$$\frac{1+\sqrt{5}}{2}.$$

---

1 ACTIVITY: Constructing a Golden Ratio

Work with a partner.

a. Use grid paper and the given scale to draw a square that is 1 unit by 1 unit. Label the midpoint of the right side of the square C. Label the bottom left corner of the square A, the bottom right corner B, and the top left corner D.

b. Draw a line from midpoint C of one side of the square to the opposite corner D.

c. Use the Pythagorean Theorem to find the length of segment CD.

d. Set the point of a compass on C. Set the compass radius to the length of segment CD. Swing the compass to intersect line BC. Label the point of intersection E. Form rectangle $ABEF$.

e. The rectangle $ABEF$ is called the *golden rectangle* because the ratio of its side lengths is the golden ratio.

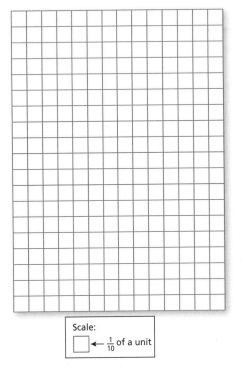

Scale:
□ ← $\frac{1}{10}$ of a unit

6.4 Simplifying Square Roots (continued)

f. Use a calculator to find a decimal approximation of the golden ratio. Round your answer to two decimal places.

---

2 ACTIVITY: The Golden Ratio and the Human Body

Work with a partner.

Leonardo da Vinci was one of the first to notice that there are several ratios in the human body that approximate the golden ratio.

a. Use a tape measure or two yardsticks to measure the lengths shown in the diagram for both you and your partner. (Take your shoes off before measuring.)

b. Record your results in the first two columns of the tables on the next page.

c. Calculate the ratios shown in the tables.

d. Leonardo da Vinci stated that for many people, the ratios are close to the golden ratio. How close are your ratios?

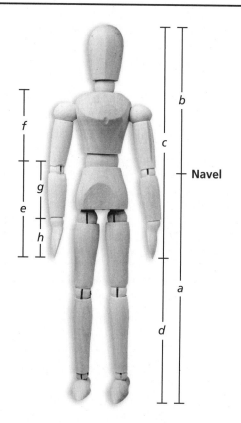

Name_____ Date _____

You		
$a =$	$b =$	$\dfrac{a}{b} =$
$c =$	$d =$	$\dfrac{c}{d} =$
$e =$	$f =$	$\dfrac{e}{f} =$
$g =$	$h =$	$\dfrac{g}{h} =$

Partner		
$a =$	$b =$	$\dfrac{a}{b} =$
$c =$	$d =$	$\dfrac{c}{d} =$
$e =$	$f =$	$\dfrac{e}{f} =$
$g =$	$h =$	$\dfrac{g}{h} =$

What Is Your Answer?

3. **IN YOUR OWN WORDS** How can you use a square root to describe the golden ratio? Use the Internet or some other reference to find examples of the golden ratio in art and architecture.

Name _____ Date _____

Simplify the expression.

1. $\dfrac{\sqrt{3}}{8} + \dfrac{1}{8}$

2. $\dfrac{2}{9} - \dfrac{\sqrt{11}}{9}$

3. $7\sqrt{7} + 3\sqrt{7}$

4. $\dfrac{3}{2}\sqrt{15} + \dfrac{1}{2}\sqrt{15}$

5. $12\sqrt{42} - 5\sqrt{42}$

6. $16.4\sqrt{21} - 15.1\sqrt{21}$

7. $\sqrt{20}$

8. $\sqrt{32}$

9. $\sqrt{75}$

10. $\sqrt{\dfrac{29}{81}}$

11. $\sqrt{\dfrac{17}{a^2}}$

12. $\sqrt{40} + 3\sqrt{10}$

13. You build a shed in your backyard.

   a. What is the perimeter of the shed?

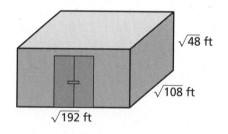

$\sqrt{48}$ ft

$\sqrt{108}$ ft

$\sqrt{192}$ ft

   b. What is the volume of the shed?

6.5 Using the Pythagorean Theorem
For use with Activity 6.5

Essential Question How can you use the Pythagorean Theorem to solve real-life problems?

1 ACTIVITY: Using the Pythagorean Theorem

Work with a partner.

a. A baseball player throws a ball from second base to home plate. How far does the player throw the ball? Include a diagram showing how you got your answer. Decide how many decimal points of accuracy are reasonable. Explain your reasoning.

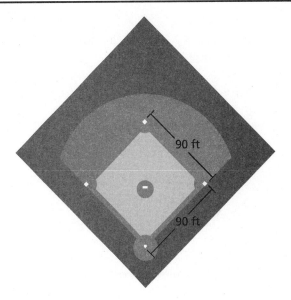

b. The distance from the pitcher's mound to home plate is 60.5 feet. Does this form a right triangle with first base? Explain your reasoning.

6.5 **Using the Pythagorean Theorem** (continued)

2 **ACTIVITY:** Firefighting and Ladders

Work with a partner.

The recommended angle for a firefighting ladder is 75°.

When a 110-foot ladder is put up against a building at this angle, the base of the ladder is about 28 feet from the building.

The base of the ladder is 8 feet above the ground.

How high on the building will the ladder reach? Round your answer to the nearest tenth.

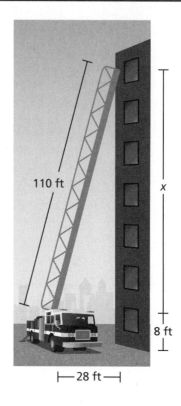

110 ft

x

8 ft

├─ 28 ft ─┤

3 **ACTIVITY:** Finding Perimeters

Work with a partner.

Find the perimeter of each figure. Round your answer to the nearest tenth. Did you use the Pythagorean Theorem? If so, explain.

a. Right triangle
b. Trapezoid
c. Parallelogram

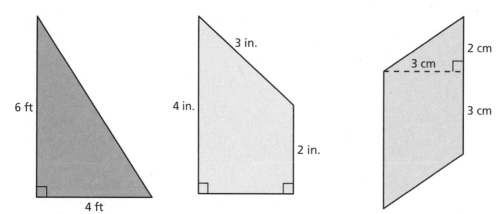

6 ft

4 ft

3 in.

4 in.

2 in.

3 cm

2 cm

3 cm

Name_____ Date _____

6.5 **Using the Pythagorean Theorem** (continued)

4 **ACTIVITY:** Writing a Formula

Work with a partner.

a. Write a formula for the area of an equilateral triangle with side length s.

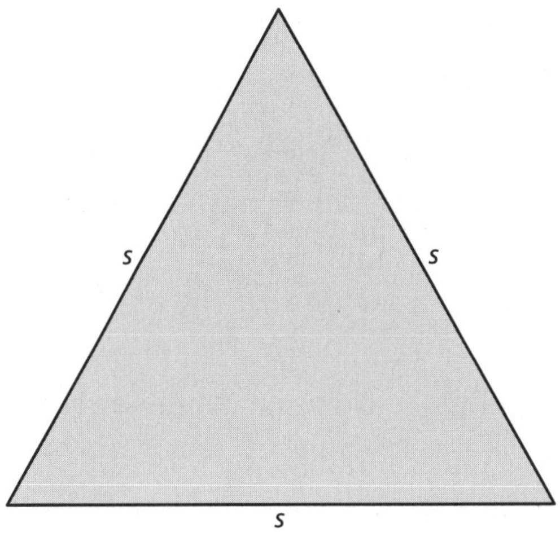

b. Use your formula to find the area of an equilateral triangle with a side length of 10 inches.

What Is Your Answer?

5. IN YOUR OWN WORDS How can you use the Pythagorean Theorem to solve real-life problems?

6. Describe a situation in which you could use the Pythagorean Theorem to help make decisions. Give an example of a real-life problem.

Name _____ Date _____

Find the distance *d*. Round your answer to the nearest tenth.

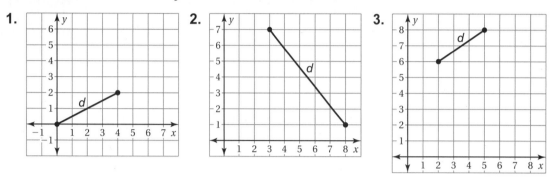

1.

2.

3.

Find the height *x*. Round your answer to the nearest tenth.

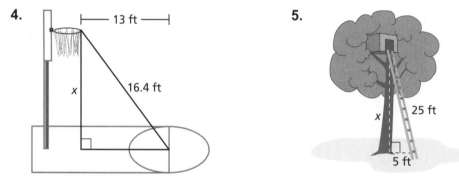

4.

5.

Tell whether the triangle with the given side lengths is a right triangle.

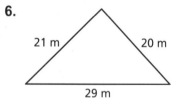

6.

21 m   20 m

29 m

7.

9 cm   7 cm

15 cm

8. You set up a badminton net in your backyard.
    About how long is the rope used to secure
    the net?

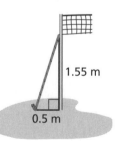

1.55 m

0.5 m

Name_____ Date_____

Use the data in the table to create a circle graph.

1.

Fabric	Percent
Polyester	68%
Rayon	28%
Spandex	4%

2.

Budget	Dollars
Bills	200
Food	100
Savings	50
Other	50

3.

Type of Lunch	Students
Sandwich	24
Pasta	16
Pizza	28
Chicken Nuggets	19
Other	13

4.

Hobbies	Students
Music	12
Collecting	4
Reading	5
Games	15
Other	9

5. You conduct a survey asking students which instrument they play. Organize the results in a circle graph.

Instruments Played	Students
Trumpet	7
Piano	15
Trombone	5
Flute	9
Saxophone	4
Drums	10
None	5

Name _____ Date _____

Use the data in the table to create a histogram.

6.

Concerts attended	Students
0–4	18
5–9	9
10–14	2

7.

Number of Puppies in Litter	Litters
0–2	1
3–5	7
6–8	12
9–11	3

8.

Boxes of Scout Cookies Sold	Scouts
0–4	9
5–9	12
10–14	20
15–19	32
20–24	28

9.

Money Raised	Students
0–19	4
20–39	6
40–59	9
60–79	8
80–99	5

10. You conduct a survey asking students how many siblings they have. Organize the results in a histogram.

Number of Siblings	Students
0–1	11
2–3	15
4–5	5
6–7	2
8–9	1

7.1 **Measures of Central Tendency**
For use with Activity 7.1

Essential Question How can you use measures of central tendency to distribute an amount evenly among a group of people?

1 **ACTIVITY:** Exploring Mean, Median, and Mode

Work with a partner. Forty-five coins are arranged in nine stacks.

5 4 3 6 2 5 8 7 5

a. Record the number of coins in each stack in a table.

Stack	1	2	3	4	5	6	7	8	9
Coins									

b. Find the mean, median, and mode of the number of coins in each stack.

c. By moving coins from one stack to another, can you change the mean? the median? the mode? Explain.

d. Is it possible to arrange the coins in stacks so that the median is 6? 8? Explain.

7.1 **Measures of Central Tendency** (continued)

2 **EXAMPLE:** Drawing a Line Plot

Work with a partner.

    a. Use the number line below. Label the tick marks from 1 to 10.

    b. Place each stack of coins in Activity 1 above the number of coins in the stack.

    c. Draw an × above each number to represent each coin in the stack. This graph is called a *line plot*.

Number of Coins

3 **ACTIVITY:** Fair and Unfair Distributions

Work with a partner.

A distribution of coins to nine people is considered *fair* if each person has the same number of coins.

    • Distribute the 45 coins into 9 stacks using a fair distribution. How is this distribution related to the mean?

    • Draw a line plot for each distribution. Which distributions seem most fair? Which distributions seem least fair? Explain your reasoning.

  a.

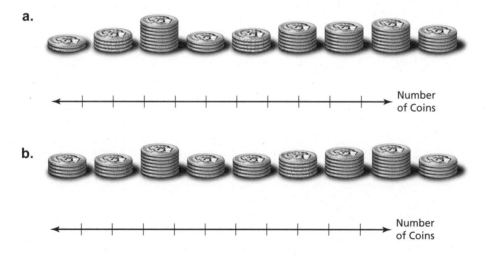

Number of Coins

  b.

Number of Coins

7.1 Measures of Central Tendency (continued)

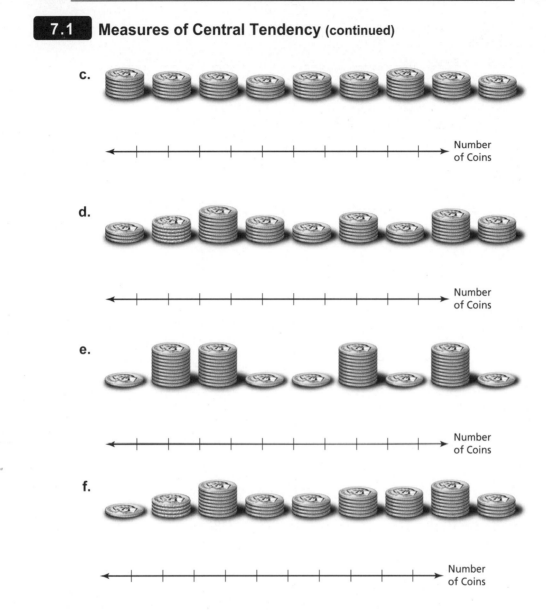

c.

Number of Coins

d.

Number of Coins

e.

Number of Coins

f.

Number of Coins

What Is Your Answer?

4. **IN YOUR OWN WORDS** How can you use measures of central tendency to distribute an amount evenly among a group of people?

5. Use the Internet or some other reference to find examples of mean or median incomes of groups of people. Describe possible distributions that could produce the given means or medians.

Name _____ Date _____

7.1 Practice
For use after Lesson 7.1

Find the mean, median, and mode of the data.

1.

Song Lengths (minutes)		
2.6	3.25	4.15
2.52	3.67	3.1
3.78	4.9	3.8

2.

$$\times$$
$$\times \quad\quad\quad\quad \times$$
$$\times \quad \times \quad \times \quad \times \quad \times \quad \times\times \quad \times \quad \times$$

1   2   3   4   5   6   7   8

Number of Books Read in a Week

Find the value of x.

3. Mean is 20; 6, 22, x, 7, 36

4. Median is 28; 16, 24, x, 48

5. A statistician records the winning scores of five basketball teams.
105, 98, 92, 108, 70

   a. Identify the outlier.

   b. Which measure of central tendency will be most affected by removing the outlier?

   c. Calculate the mean and median with and without the outlier.

7.2 **Box-and-Whisker Plots**
For use with Activity 7.2

Essential Question How can you use a box-and-whisker plot to describe a population?

1 ACTIVITY: Drawing a Box-and-Whisker Plot

Work with a partner.

The numbers of first cousins of each student in an eighth-grade class are shown.

A box-and-whisker plot uses a number line to represent the data visually.

Numbers of First Cousins			
3	10	18	8
9	3	0	32
23	19	13	8
6	3	3	10
12	45	1	5
13	24	16	14

a. Order the data set and write it on a strip of grid paper with 24 equally spaced boxes.

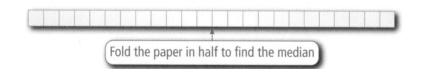

Fold the paper in half to find the median

b. Fold the paper in half again to divide the data into four groups. Because there are 24 numbers in the data set, each group should have six numbers.

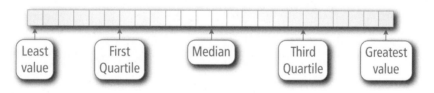

Least value   First Quartile   Median   Third Quartile   Greatest value

c. Use the number line. Graph the five numbers that you found in part (b).

7.2 **Box-and-Whisker Plots** (continued)

d. Explain how the box-and-whisker plot shown below represents the data set.

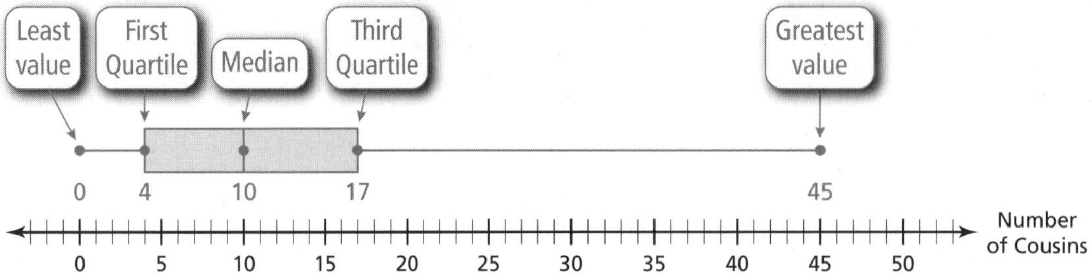

2 ACTIVITY: Conducting a Survey

Conduct a survey in your class. Ask each student to write the number of his or her first cousins on a piece of paper.

Two people are first cousins if they share at least one grandparent, but do not share a parent.

Collect the pieces of paper and write the data on the chalkboard.

Now, work with a partner to draw a box-and-whisker plot of the data.

7.2 Box-and-Whisker Plots (continued)

3 **ACTIVITY:** Reading a Box-and-Whisker Plot

Work with a partner. The box-and-whisker plots show the test score
distributions of two eighth-grade standardized tests. The tests were taken
by the same group of students. One test was taken in the fall and the other
was taken in the spring.

a. Compare and contrast the test results.

b. Decide which box-and-whisker plot represents the results of which test.
How did you make your decision?

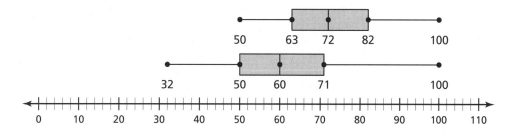

What Is Your Answer?

4. **IN YOUR OWN WORDS** How can you use a box-and-whisker plot to
describe test scores?

5. Describe who might be interested in test score distributions like those
shown in Activity 3. Explain why it is important for such people to
know test score distributions.

Name _____ Date _____

Make a box-and-whisker plot for the data.

1. Hours of reading: 1, 6, 7, 5, 5, 8, 4, 8

2. Golf scores: −5, −12, 0, 2, −4, 3, −3, −7, −1, −3, −5, 0

3. The table shows quiz scores of 10 students. Make a box-and-whisker plot for the data. What does the box-and-whisker plot tell you about the data?

Quiz Scores (points)	
20	19
17	18
16	18
22	20
24	25

4. The box-and-whisker plot shows the number of pages in a stack of books. What is the range of the lower 25% of the data?

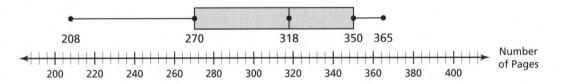

Name_____ Date_____

7.3 Scatter Plots and Lines of Best Fit
For use with Activity 7.3

Essential Question How can you use data to predict an event?

---

1 ACTIVITY: Representing Data by a Linear Equation

Work with a partner. You have been working on a science project for
8 months. Each month, you have measured the length of a baby alligator.

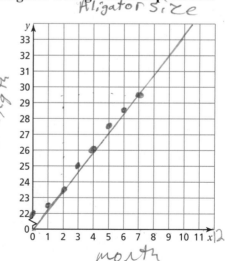

The table shows your measurements.

$2\overline{)\begin{array}{c}2.5\\5.0\\4.6\\\hline 10\end{array}}$

September⁹   April⁴

Month, x	0	1	2	3	4	5	6	7
Length (in.), y	22.0	22.5	23.5	25.0	26.0	27.5	28.5	29.5

Use the following steps to predict the baby alligator's length next September.

$\dfrac{6}{5} \cdot \dfrac{12}{1} = \dfrac{72}{5}$

$14\dfrac{2}{5}$

a. Graph the data in the table.

b. Draw the straight line that you think best approximates the points.

$\dfrac{6}{5}$

c. Write an equation of the line you drew.

$$y = \dfrac{6}{5}x + 21$$

d. Use the equation to predict the baby alligator's length next September.

37.5

Aligator size

7.3 **Scatter Plots and Lines of Best Fit** (continued)

2 ACTIVITY: Representing Data by a Linear Equation

Work with a partner. You are a biologist and are studying bat populations.

You are asked to predict the number of bats that will be living in an abandoned mine in 3 years.

To start, you find the number of bats that have been living in the mine during the past 8 years.

The table shows the results of your research.

7 years ago							this year

Year, *x*	0	1	2	3	4	5	6	7
Bats (thousands), *y*	327	306	299	270	254	232	215	197

Use the following steps to predict the number of bats that will be living in the mine after 3 years.

a. Graph the data in the table.

b. Draw the straight line that you think best approximates the points.

c. Write an equation of the line you drew.

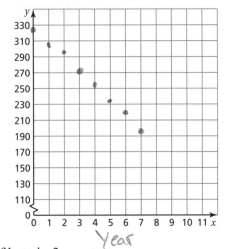

Bats

Year

d. Use the equation to predict the number of bats in 3 years.

7.3 **Scatter Plots and Line of Best Fit** (continued)

What Is Your Answer?

3. **IN YOUR OWN WORDS** How can you use data to predict an event?

4. Use the Internet or some other reference to find data that appear to have a linear pattern. List the data in a table and graph the data. Use an equation that is based on the data to predict a future event.

Name _____ Date _____

Tell whether the data show a *positive*, a *negative* or *no* relationship.

1.

2.

3.

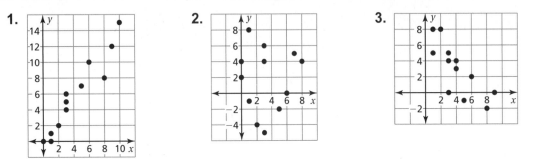

4. The scatter plot shows the participation in a bowling league over eight years.

   a. About how many people were in the league in 2004?

   b. Describe the relationship shown by the data.

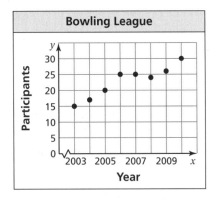

5. The table shows the money you owe to pay off a credit card bill over five months.

   a. Make a scatter plot of the data.

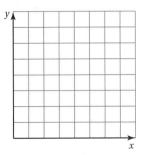

Months, x	Money owed (dollars), y
1	1200
2	1000
3	850
4	600
5	410

   b. Draw a line of best fit.

   c. Write an equation for the line of best fit.

   d. Predict the amount of money you will owe in six months.

Name_____ Date _____

7.3b **Practice**
For use after Lesson 7.3b

1. You randomly survey students in a school about whether they got the flu after receiving a flu shot. The results of the survey are shown in the two-way table.

		Flu Shot	
		Yes	No
Flu	Yes	8	13
	No	27	32

   a. How many of the students in the survey received a flu shot and still got the flu?

   b. Find and interpret the sum of the entries in each row and column.

		Flu Shot		
		Yes	No	Total
Flu	Yes	8	13	
	No	27	32	
	Total			

   c. What percent of the students in the survey did not get a flu shot and did not get the flu?

7.3b **Practice** (continued)

2. You randomly survey students in a school about whether they eat breakfast at home or at school.

   Grade 6 Students: 28 eat breakfast at home, 12 eat breakfast at school

   Grade 7 Students: 15 eat breakfast at home, 15 eat breakfast at school

   Grade 8 Students: 9 eat breakfast at home, 21 eat breakfast at school

   a. Make a two-way table including the totals of the rows and columns.

   b. For each grade level, what percent of the students in the survey eat breakfast at home? eat lunch at school? Organize the results in a two-way table. Explain what one of the entries represents.

   c. Does the table in part (b) show a relationship between grade level and breakfast choice? Explain.

Name_____ Date_____

7.4 Choosing a Data Display
For use with Activity 7.4

Essential Question How can you display data in a way that helps you make decisions?

1 ACTIVITY: Displaying Data

Work with a partner. Analyze and display each data set in a way that best describes the data. Explain your choice of display.

a. **ROAD KILL** A group of schools in New England participated in a 2-month study and reported 3962 dead animals.

Birds 307
Mammals 2746
Amphibians 145
Reptiles 75
Unknown 689

b. **BLACK BEAR ROAD KILL** The data below show the number of black bears killed on Florida roads from 1987 to 2006.

1987	30	1997	74
1988	37	1998	88
1989	46	1999	82
1990	33	2000	109
1991	43	2001	99
1992	35	2002	129
1993	43	2003	111
1994	47	2004	127
1995	49	2005	141
1996	61	2006	135

7.4 Choosing a Data Display (continued)

c. **RACCOON ROAD KILL** A 1-week study along a 4-mile section of road found the following weights (in pounds) of raccoons that had been killed by vehicles.

13.4	14.8	17.0	12.9	21.3	21.5	16.8	14.8
15.2	18.7	18.6	17.2	18.5	9.4	19.4	15.7
14.5	9.5	25.4	21.5	17.3	19.1	11.0	12.4
20.4	13.6	17.5	18.5	21.5	14.0	13.9	19.0

d. What do you think can be done to minimize the number of animals killed by vehicles?

---

2 **ACTIVITY:** Statistics Project

ENDANGERED SPECIES PROJECT Use the Internet or some other reference to write a report about an animal species that is (or has been) endangered. Include graphical displays of the data you have gathered.

Sample: Florida Key Deer In 1939, Florida banned the hunting of Key deer. The numbers of Key deer fell to about 100 in the 1940s.

About half of Key deer deaths are due to vehicles.

7.4 **Choosing a Data Display** (continued)

In 1947, public sentiment was stirred by 11-year-old Glenn Allen from Miami. Allen organized Boy Scouts and others in a letter-writing campaign that led to the establishment of the National Key Deer Refuge in 1957. The approximately 8600-acre refuge includes 2280 acres of designated wilderness.

Key Deer Refuge has increased the population of Key deer. A recent study estimated the total Key deer population to be between 700 and 800.

One of two Key deer wildlife underpasses on Big Pine Key.

What Is Your Answer?

3. **IN YOUR OWN WORDS** How can you display data in a way that helps you make decisions? Use the Internet or some other reference to find examples of the following types of data displays.

- Bar graph
- Circle graph
- Scatter plot

- Stem-and-leaf plot
- Box-and-whisker plot

Name _____ Date _____

Practice
For use after Lesson 7.4

Choose an appropriate data display for the situation. Explain your reasoning.

1. the number of people that donated blood over the last 5 years

2. percent of class participating in school clubs

Explain why the data display is misleading.

3.

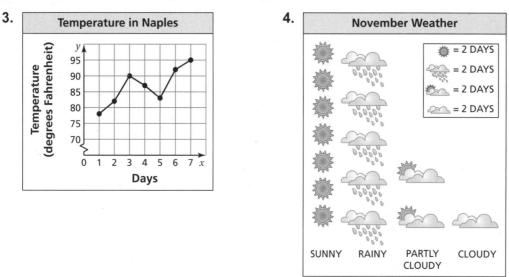

4.

5. A team statistician wants to use a data display to show the points scored per game during the season. Choose an appropriate data display for the situation. Explain your reasoning.

Chapter 8 **Fair Game Review**

Complete the number sentence with <, >, or =.

1. $\dfrac{3}{4}$ _____ 0.2

2. $\dfrac{7}{10}$ _____ 0.7

3. -0.6 _____ $-\dfrac{2}{3}$

4. $\sqrt{3}$ _____ 1.75

5. $\sqrt{12}$ _____ 6

6. 1.8 _____ $\dfrac{31}{16}$

7. Your height is 5 feet and $1\dfrac{5}{8}$ inches. Your friend's height is 5.6 feet. Who is taller? Explain.

Chapter 8 Fair Game Review (continued)

Graph the inequality.

8. $x < -3$

9. $x \geq -5$

10. $x \leq 2$

11. $x > 7$

12. $x \leq -2.3$

13. $x > \dfrac{2}{5}$

14. The deepest free dive by a human in the ocean is 417 feet. The depth humans have been in the ocean can be represented by the inequality $x \leq 417$. Graph the inequality.

Name_____ Date_____

8.1 Writing and Graphing Inequalities
For use with Activity 8.1

Essential Question How can you use an inequality to describe a real-life statement?

---

1 ACTIVITY: Writing and Graphing Inequalities

Work with a partner. Write an inequality for the statement. Then sketch the graph of all the numbers that make the inequality true.

a. **Statement:** The temperature t in Minot, North Dakota has never been below $-36°F$.

Inequality: _____

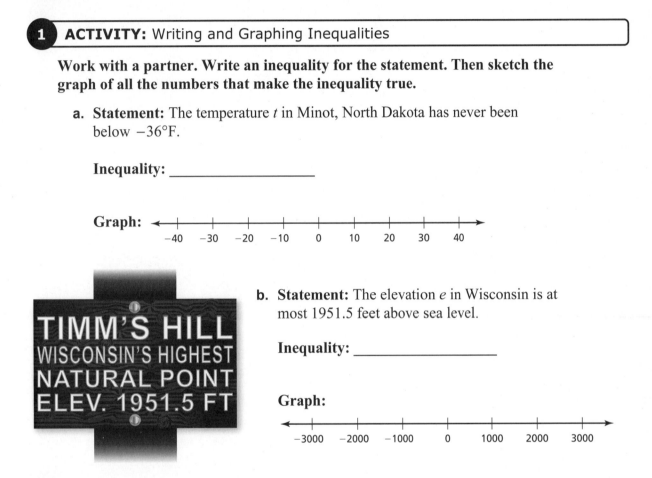

Graph:

$$\begin{array}{ccccccccc} -40 & -30 & -20 & -10 & 0 & 10 & 20 & 30 & 40 \end{array}$$

b. **Statement:** The elevation e in Wisconsin is at most 1951.5 feet above sea level.

Inequality: _____

Graph:

$$\begin{array}{ccccccc} -3000 & -2000 & -1000 & 0 & 1000 & 2000 & 3000 \end{array}$$

TIMM'S HILL
WISCONSIN'S HIGHEST
NATURAL POINT
ELEV. 1951.5 FT

---

2 ACTIVITY: Writing and Graphing Inequalities

Work with a partner. Write an inequality for the graph. Then, in words, describe all the values of x that make the inequality true.

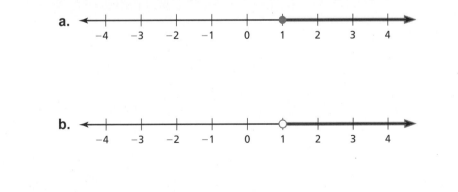

a.
$$\begin{array}{ccccccccc} -4 & -3 & -2 & -1 & 0 & 1 & 2 & 3 & 4 \end{array}$$

b.
$$\begin{array}{ccccccccc} -4 & -3 & -2 & -1 & 0 & 1 & 2 & 3 & 4 \end{array}$$

8.1 **Writing and Graphing Inequalities** (continued)

c.
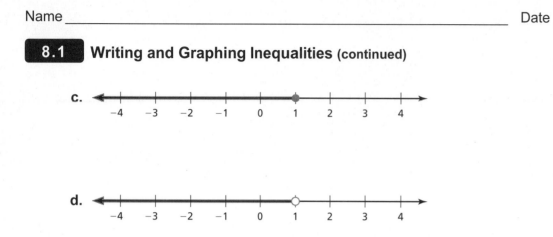

d.

---

3 **ACTIVITY:** Triangle Inequality

Work with a partner. Use 8 to 10 pieces of spaghetti.

- Break one piece of spaghetti into three parts that can be used to form a triangle.

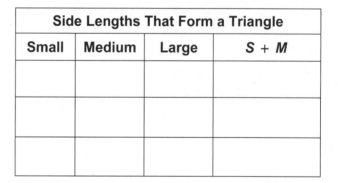

- Form a triangle and use a centimeter ruler to measure each side. Round the side lengths to the nearest tenth.

- Record the side lengths in the table.

Side Lengths That Form a Triangle			
Small	Medium	Large	S + M

- Repeat the process with two other pieces of spaghetti.

- Repeat the experiment by breaking pieces of spaghetti into three pieces that *do not* form a triangle. Record the lengths in a table.

Side Lengths That Do Not Form a Triangle			
Small	Medium	Large	S + M

8.1   Writing and Graphing Inequalities (continued)

- **INDUCTIVE REASONING** Write a rule that uses an inequality to compare the lengths of three sides of a triangle.

- Use your rule to decide whether the following triangles are possible. Explain.

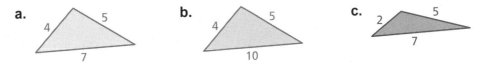

a.   4   5   7

b.   4   5   10

c.   2   5   7

What Is Your Answer?

4. **IN YOUR OWN WORDS** How can you use an inequality to describe a real-life statement? Give two examples of real-life statements that can be represented by inequalities.

Name _____ Date _____

Write the word sentence as an inequality.

1. A number p is no greater than -6.

2. A number n divided by -2 is no less than $\frac{1}{2}$.

Tell whether the given value is a solution of the inequality.

3. $q + 7 \geq 8;\ q = 10$

4. $-12r < -6;\ r = -2$

5. $-2.4k \geq -4;\ k = 0.5$

6. $\frac{x}{4} < x - 9;\ x = 8$

Graph the inequality on a number line.

7. $p \leq 4\frac{1}{2}$

8. $z > -8.3$

9. For your birthday, you want to invite some friends to join you at the movies. Movie tickets cost \$8. You can spend no more than \$35. Write an inequality to represent this situation. Then solve the inequality to find the greatest number of people you can invite.

Name_____ Date_____

 8.2 **Solving Inequalities Using Addition or Subtraction**
For use with Activity 8.2

Essential Question How can you use addition or subtraction to solve an inequality?

1 **ACTIVITY:** Quarterback Passing Efficiency

Work with a partner. The National Collegiate Athletic Association (NCAA) uses the following formula to rank the passing efficiency P of quarterbacks.

$$P = \frac{8.4Y + 100C + 330T - 200N}{A}$$

Y = total length of all completed passes (in **Y**ards)
C = **C**ompleted passes
T = passes resulting in a **T**ouchdown
N = i**N**tercepted passes
A = **A**ttempted passes
M = inco**M**plete passes

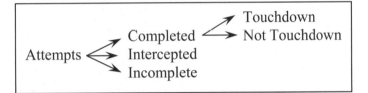

Which of the following equations or inequalities are true relationships among the variables? **Explain your reasoning.**

 a. $C + N < A$ **b.** $C + N \leq A$ **c.** $T < C$ **d.** $T \leq C$

 e. $N < A$ **f.** $A > T$ **g.** $A - C \geq M$ **h.** $A = C + N + M$

8.2 **Solving Inequalities Using Addition or Subtraction** (continued)

2 **ACTIVITY:** Quarterback Passing Efficiency

Work with a partner. Which of the following quarterbacks has a passing efficiency rating that satisfies the inequality $P > 100$? Show your work.

Player	Attempts	Completions	Yards	Touchdowns	Interceptions
A	149	88	1065	7	9
B	400	205	2000	10	3
C	426	244	3105	30	9
D	188	89	1167	6	15

3 **ACTIVITY:** Finding Solutions of Inequalities

Work with a partner. Use the passing efficiency formula to create a passing record that makes the inequality true. Then describe the values of P that make the inequality true.

  a. $P < 0$

Attempts	Completions	Yards	Touchdowns	Interceptions

  b. $P + 100 \geq 250$

Attempts	Completions	Yards	Touchdowns	Interceptions

  c. $180 < P - 50$

Attempts	Completions	Yards	Touchdowns	Interceptions

8.2 **Solving Inequalities Using Addition or Subtraction** (continued)

d. $P + 30 \geq 120$

Attempts	Completions	Yards	Touchdowns	Interceptions

e. $P - 250 > -80$

Attempts	Completions	Yards	Touchdowns	Interceptions

What Is Your Answer?

4. Write a rule that describes how to solve inequalities like those in Activity 3. Then use your rule to solve each of the inequalities in Activity 3.

5. **IN YOUR OWN WORDS** How can you use addition or subtraction to solve an inequality?

6. How is solving the inequality $x + 3 < 4$ similar to solving the equation $x + 3 = 4$? How is it different?

8.2 Practice
For use after Lesson 8.2

Solve the inequality. Graph the solution.

1. $x - 4 < 8$

2. $16 + p \geq 14$

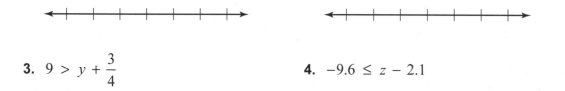

3. $9 > y + \dfrac{3}{4}$

4. $-9.6 \leq z - 2.1$

Write and solve an inequality that represents the value of x.

5. The perimeter is less than 15 feet.

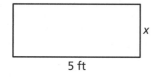

5 ft

6. The height is greater than the base.

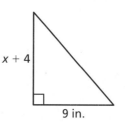

$x + 4$

9 in.

7. Your goal is to sell at least 50 boxes of cookies for your school fundraiser.

   a. Write an inequality that represents your goal.

   b. You sell 26 boxes. Write and solve a new inequality to represent how many boxes you need to sell to reach your goal.

8.3 **Solving Inequalities Using Multiplication or Division**
For use with Activity 8.3

Essential Question How can you use multiplication or division to solve
an inequality?

1 **ACTIVITY:** Using a Table to Solve an Inequality

Work with a partner.

- **Complete the table.**
- **Decide which graph represents the solution of the inequality.**
- **Write the solution of the inequality.**

a. $3x \le 6$

x	−1	0	1	2	3	4	5
3x							
3x $\overset{?}{\le}$ 6							

b. $-2x > 4$

x	−5	−4	−3	−2	−1	0	1
−2x							
−2x $\overset{?}{>}$ 4							

8.3 **Solving Inequalities Using Multiplication or Division** (continued)

2 **ACTIVITY:** Writing a Rule

Work with a partner. Use a table to solve each inequality.

a. $3x > 3$ **b.** $4x \leq 4$ **c.** $-2x \geq 6$ **d.** $-5x < 10$

x									
$3x$									
$4x$									
$-2x$									
$-5x$									

Write a rule that describes how to solve inequalities like those in Activity 1.
Then use your rule to solve each of the four inequalities above.

3 **ACTIVITY:** Using a Table to Solve an Inequality

Work with a partner.

- Complete the table.

- Decide which graph represents the solution of the inequality.

- Write the solution of the inequality.

a. $\dfrac{x}{2} \geq 1$

x	-1	0	1	2	3	4	5
$\dfrac{x}{2}$							
$\dfrac{x}{2} \overset{?}{\geq} 1$							

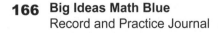

Name_____ Date_____

b. $\dfrac{x}{-3} < \dfrac{2}{3}$

x	-5	-4	-3	-2	-1	0	1
$\dfrac{x}{-3}$							
$\dfrac{x}{-3} \overset{?}{<} \dfrac{2}{3}$							

---

4 **ACTIVITY:** Writing a Rule

Work with a partner. Use a table to solve each inequality.

a. $\dfrac{x}{4} \geq 1$ **b.** $\dfrac{x}{2} < \dfrac{3}{2}$ **c.** $\dfrac{x}{-2} > 2$ **d.** $\dfrac{x}{-5} \leq \dfrac{1}{5}$

x									
$\dfrac{x}{4}$									
$\dfrac{x}{2}$									
$\dfrac{x}{-2}$									
$\dfrac{x}{-5}$									

Write a rule that describes how to solve inequalities like those in Activity 3.
Then use your rule to solve each of the four inequalities above.

What Is Your Answer?

5. IN YOUR OWN WORDS How can you use multiplication or division to
solve an inequality?

Name _____ Date _____

Solve the inequality. Graph the solution.

1. $5n < 75$

2. $\dfrac{x}{6} \le -12$

3. $-15t > -60$

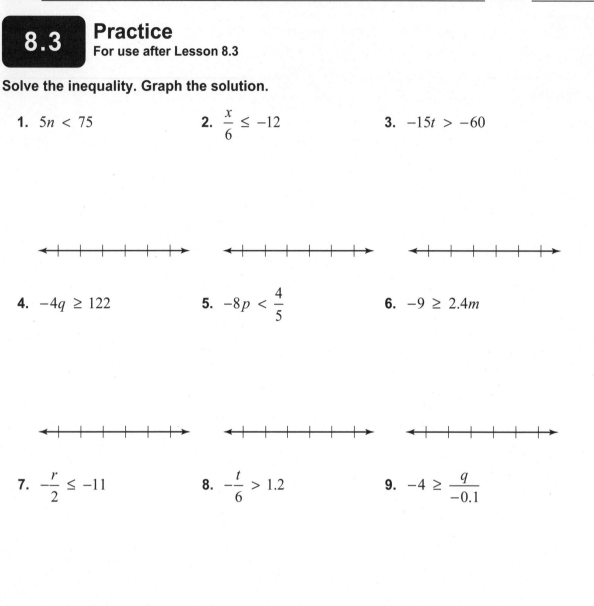

4. $-4q \ge 122$

5. $-8p < \dfrac{4}{5}$

6. $-9 \ge 2.4m$

7. $-\dfrac{r}{2} \le -11$

8. $-\dfrac{t}{6} > 1.2$

9. $-4 \ge \dfrac{q}{-0.1}$

10. To win a trivia game, you need at least 60 points. Each question is worth 4 points. Write and solve an inequality that represents the number of questions you need to answer correctly to win the game.

8.4 Solving Multi-Step Inequalities
For use with Activity 8.4

Essential Question How can you use an inequality to describe the area and perimeter of a composite figure?

---

1 ACTIVITY: Areas and Perimeters of Composite Figures

Work with a partner.

a. For what values of x will the area of the shaded region be greater than 12 square units?

b. For what values of x will the sum of the inner and outer perimeters of the shaded region be greater than 20 units?

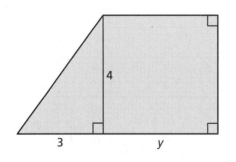

c. For what values of y will the area of the trapezoid be less than or equal to 10 square units?

d. For what values of y will the perimeter of the trapezoid be less than or equal to 16 units?

8.4 **Solving Multi-Step Inequalities** (continued)

e. For what values of w will the area of the shaded region be greater than or equal to 36 square units?

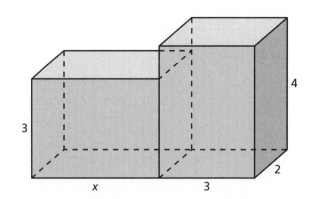

f. For what values of w will the sum of the inner and outer perimeters of the shaded region be greater than 47 units?

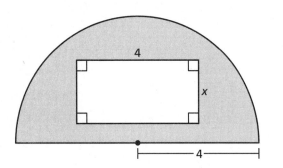

g. For what values of x will the area of the shaded region be less than 4π square units?

h. For what values of x will the sum of the inner and outer perimeters of the shaded region be less than $4\pi + 20$ units?

2 **ACTIVITY:** Volume and Surface Area of a Composite Solid

Work with a partner.

a. For what values of x will the volume of the solid be greater than or equal to 42 cubic units?

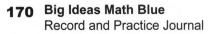

b. For what values of x will the surface area of the solid be greater than 72 square units?

8.4 Solving Multi-Step Inequalities (continued)

3 ACTIVITY: Planning a Budget

Work with a partner.

You are building a patio. You want to cover the patio with Spanish tile that costs $5 per square foot. Your budget for the tile is $1700. How wide can you make the patio without going over your budget?

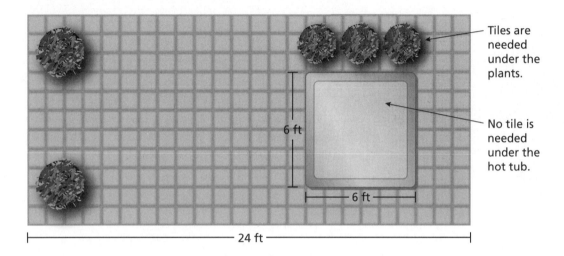

Tiles are needed under the plants.

6 ft

No tile is needed under the hot tub.

6 ft

24 ft

What Is Your Answer?

4. **IN YOUR OWN WORDS** How can you use an inequality to describe the area and perimeter of a composite figure? Give an example. Include a diagram with your example.

Name _____ Date _____

Solve the inequality. Graph the solution.

1. $9x - 6 > 66$

2. $\dfrac{d}{3} + 7 \le -11$

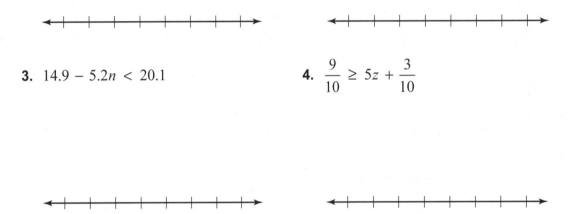

3. $14.9 - 5.2n < 20.1$

4. $\dfrac{9}{10} \ge 5z + \dfrac{3}{10}$

5. $8(p + 3) > -24$

6. $-\dfrac{1}{2}(y + 8) < -12$

7. In the United States music industry, an album is awarded gold certification with at least 500,000 albums sold. A recording artist is selling about 1200 albums each day. The artist has already sold 15,000 albums. About how many more days will it take before the album is awarded gold certification?

Name_____ Date_____

Find the sum or difference.

1. $8.01 + 4.2$

2. $9.736 + 10.922$

3. $4.81 + 0.755$

4. $10.6 - 2.18$

5. $6.75 - 5.9$

6. $3.874 - 0.06$

7. You bring $20 on a shopping trip. You buy a shirt for $7.62.

   a. How much money do you have after you buy the shirt?

   b. Later, you buy a hat for $5.18. How much money do you have after you buy the hat?

8. You have 3.85 yards of fleece and 2.6 yards of silk for your design supplies. How many total yards of fabric do you have?

Chapter 9 **Fair Game Review** (continued)

Find the product or quotient.

9. 3.92 • 0.6

10. 0.78 • 0.13

11. 5.004
   × 1.2

12. 6.3 ÷ 0.7

13. 2.25 ÷ 1.5

14. 0.003)‾8.1

15. Grapes cost $1.98 per pound. You buy 3.5 pounds of grapes. How much do you pay for the grapes?

16. A box of cereal costs $3.69. The box has 13.7 ounces of cereal. About how much does each ounce cost?

Name_____ Date_____

9.1 Exponents
For use with Activity 9.1

Essential Question How can you use exponents to write numbers?

The expression 3^5 is called a **power.** The **base** is 3. The **exponent** is 5.

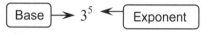

1 ACTIVITY: Using Exponent Notation

Work with a partner.

   a. Complete the table.

Power	Repeated Multiplication Form	Value
$(-3)^1$		
$(-3)^2$		
$(-3)^3$		
$(-3)^4$		
$(-3)^5$		
$(-3)^6$		
$(-3)^7$		

   b. Describe what is meant by the expression $(-3)^n$. How can you find the

      value of $(-3)^n$?

Name _____ Date _____

2 **ACTIVITY:** Using Exponent Notation

Work with a partner.

a. The cube at the right has $3 in each of its small cubes. Write a single power that represents the total amount of money in the large cube.

b. Evaluate the power to find the total amount of money in the large cube.

3 **ACTIVITY:** Writing Powers as Whole Numbers

Work with a partner. Write each distance as a whole number. Which numbers do you know how to write in words? For instance, in words, 10^3 is equal to _one thousand_.

a. 10^{26} meters:
Diameter of observable universe

b. 10^{21} meters:
Diameter of Milky Way Galaxy

c. 10^{16} meters:
Diameter of Solar System

d. 10^7 meters:
Diameter of Earth

e. 10^6 meters:
Length of Lake Erie Shoreline

f. 10^5 meters:
Width of Lake Erie

Name_____ Date _____

9.1 Exponents (continued)

4 ACTIVITY: Writing a Power

Work with a partner. Write the number of kits, cats, sacks, and wives as a power.

As I was going to St. Ives
I met a man with seven wives
and every wife had seven sacks
and every sack had seven cats
and every cat had seven kits
Kits, cats, sacks, wives
How many were going to St. Ives?

Nursery Rhyme, 1730

What Is Your Answer?

5. **IN YOUR OWN WORDS** How can you use exponents to write numbers? Give some examples of how exponents are used in real life.

Name _____ Date _____

9.1 **Practice**
For use after Lesson 9.1

Write the product using exponents.

1. $4 \cdot 4 \cdot 4 \cdot 4 \cdot 4$

2. $\left(-\dfrac{1}{8}\right) \cdot \left(-\dfrac{1}{8}\right) \cdot \left(-\dfrac{1}{8}\right)$

3. $5 \cdot 5 \cdot (-x) \cdot (-x) \cdot (-x) \cdot (-x)$

4. $9 \cdot 9 \cdot y \cdot y \cdot y \cdot y \cdot y \cdot y$

Evaluate the expression.

5. 10^3

6. $(-7)^4$

7. $-\left(\dfrac{1}{6}\right)^5$

8. $3 + 6 \cdot (-5)^2$

9. $\left| -\dfrac{1}{3}\left(1^{10} + 9 - 2^3\right) \right|$

10. A foam toy is 2 inches wide. It doubles in size for every minute it is in water. Write an expression for the width of the toy after 5 minutes. What is the width after 5 minutes?

Name_____ Date _____

9.2 Product of Powers Property
For use with Activity 9.2

Essential Question How can you multiply two powers that have the same base?

> **1 ACTIVITY:** Finding Products of Powers

Work with a partner.

a. Complete the table.

Product	Repeated Multiplication Form	Power
$2^2 \cdot 2^4$		
$(-3)^2 \cdot (-3)^4$		
$7^3 \cdot 7^2$		
$5.1^1 \cdot 5.1^6$		
$(-4)^2 \cdot (-4)^2$		
$10^3 \cdot 10^5$		
$\left(\dfrac{1}{2}\right)^5 \cdot \left(\dfrac{1}{2}\right)^5$		

b. **INDUCTIVE REASONING** Describe the pattern in the table. Then write a rule for multiplying two powers that have the same base.

$$a^m \cdot a^n = a \text{———}$$

c. Use your rule to simplify the products in the first column of the table above. Does your rule give the results in the third column?

9.2   Product of Powers Property (continued)

2   ACTIVITY: Using a Calculator

Work with a partner.

Some calculators have *exponent keys* that are used to evaluate powers.

Use a calculator with an exponent key to evaluate the products in Activity 1.

3   ACTIVITY: The Penny Puzzle

Work with a partner.

- The rows y and columns x of a chess board are numbered as shown.

- Each position on the chess board has a stack of pennies. (Only the first row is shown.)

- The number of pennies in each stack is $2^x \cdot 2^y$.

a. How many pennies are in the stack in location $(3, 5)$?

9.2 **Product of Powers Property** (continued)

b. Which locations have 32 pennies in their stacks?

c. How much money (in dollars) is in the location with the tallest stack?

d. A penny is about 0.06 inch thick. About how tall (in inches) is the tallest stack?

What Is Your Answer?

4. IN YOUR OWN WORDS How can you multiply two powers that have the same base? Give two examples of your rule.

Big Ideas Math Blue **181**
Record and Practice Journal

Name _____ Date _____

Simplify the expression. Write your answer as a power.

1. $(-6)^5 \bullet (-6)^4$

2. $x^1 \bullet x^9$

3. $\left(\dfrac{4}{5}\right)^3 \bullet \left(\dfrac{4}{5}\right)^{12}$

4. $(-1.5)^{11} \bullet (-1.5)^{11}$

5. $\left(y^{10}\right)^{20}$

6. $\left(\left(-\dfrac{2}{9}\right)^8\right)^7$

Simplify the expression.

7. $(2a)^6$

8. $(-4b)^4$

9. $\left(-\dfrac{9}{10}p\right)^2$

10. $(xy)^{15}$

11. $10^5 \bullet 10^3 - \left(10^1\right)^8$

12. $7^2\left(7^4 \bullet 7^4\right)$

13. The surface area of the sun is about $4 \times 3.141 \times \left(7 \times 10^5\right)^2$ square kilometers. Simplify the expression.

Name_____ Date_____

9.3 Quotient of Powers Property
For use with Activity 9.3

Essential Question   How can you divide two powers that have the same base?

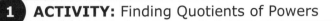

1 **ACTIVITY:** Finding Quotients of Powers

Work with a partner.

a. Complete the table.

Quotient	Repeated Multiplication Form	Power
$\dfrac{2^4}{2^2}$		
$\dfrac{(-4)^5}{(-4)^2}$		
$\dfrac{7^7}{7^3}$		
$\dfrac{8.5^9}{8.5^6}$		
$\dfrac{10^8}{10^5}$		
$\dfrac{3^{12}}{3^4}$		
$\dfrac{(-5)^7}{(-5)^5}$		
$\dfrac{11^4}{11^1}$		

b. **INDUCTIVE REASONING** Describe the pattern in the table. Then write a rule for dividing two powers that have the same base.

$$\frac{a^m}{a^n} = a^{\underline{\quad\quad}}$$

9.3 **Quotient of Powers Property** (continued)

    c. Use your rule to simplify the quotients in the first column of the table on the previous page. Does your rule give the results in the third column?

---

2 **ACTIVITY:** Comparing Volumes

Work with a partner.

How many of the smaller cubes will fit inside the larger cube? Record your results in the table on the next page. Describe the pattern in the table.

    a. Sample:

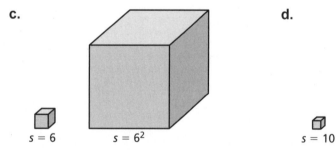

$s = 4$ $s = 4^2$

    b.

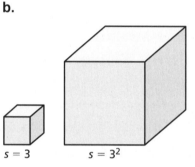

$s = 3$ $s = 3^2$

    c.

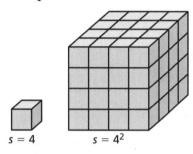

$s = 6$ $s = 6^2$

    d.

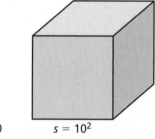

$s = 10$ $s = 10^2$

9.3 Quotient of Powers Property (continued)

	Volume of Smaller Cube	Volume of Larger Cube	$\dfrac{\text{Larger Volume}}{\text{Smaller Volume}}$	Answer
a.				
b.				
c.				
d.				

What Is Your Answer?

3. **IN YOUR OWN WORDS** How can you divide two powers that have the same base? Give two examples of your rule.

Name_____ Date _____

Simplify the expression. Write your answer as a power.

1. $\dfrac{7^6}{7^5}$

2. $\dfrac{(-21)^{15}}{(-21)^9}$

3. $\dfrac{8.6^{11}}{8.6^4}$

4. $\dfrac{(3.9)^{20}}{(3.9)^{10}}$

5. $\dfrac{t^7}{t^3}$

6. $\dfrac{d^{32}}{d^{16}}$

7. $\dfrac{8^7 \cdot 8^4}{8^9}$

8. $\dfrac{(-1.1)^{13} \cdot (-1.1)^{12}}{(-1.1)^{10} \cdot (-1.1)^1}$

9. $\dfrac{m^{50}}{m^{22}} \cdot \dfrac{m^{17}}{m^{15}}$

Simplify the expression.

10. $\dfrac{k \cdot 3^9}{3^5}$

11. $\dfrac{x^4 \cdot y^{10} \cdot 2^{11}}{y^8 \cdot 2^7}$

12. $\dfrac{a^{15}b^{19}}{a^6b^{12}}$

13. The radius of a basketball is about 3.6 times greater than the radius of a tennis ball. How many times greater is the volume of a basketball than the volume of a tennis ball? $\left(\text{Note: The volume of a sphere is } V = \dfrac{4}{3}\pi r^3. \right)$

9.4 Zero and Negative Exponents
For use with Activity 9.4

Essential Question How can you define zero and negative exponents?

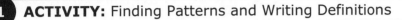
1 **ACTIVITY:** Finding Patterns and Writing Definitions

Work with a partner.

a. Talk about the following notation.

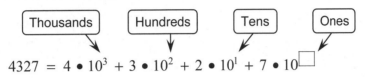

$$4327 = 4 \cdot 10^3 + 3 \cdot 10^2 + 2 \cdot 10^1 + 7 \cdot 10^{\square}$$

What patterns do you see in the first three exponents?

Continue the pattern to find the fourth exponent.

How would you define 10^0? Explain.

b. Complete the table.

n	5	4	3	2	1	0
2^n						

c. Use the Quotient of Powers Property to complete the table.

$\dfrac{3^5}{3^2} = 3^{5-2} =$		$=$
$\dfrac{3^4}{3^2} = 3^{4-2} =$		$=$
$\dfrac{3^3}{3^2} = 3^{3-2} =$		$=$
$\dfrac{3^2}{3^2} = 3^{2-2} =$		$=$

9.4 **Zero and Negative Exponents** (continued)

What patterns do you see in the first four rows of the table on the previous page? How would you define 3^0? Explain.

---

2 **ACTIVITY:** Comparing Volumes

Work with a partner.

The quotients show three ratios of the volumes of the solids. Identify each ratio, find its value, and describe what it means.

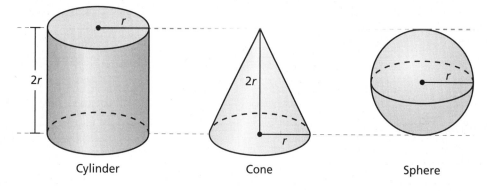

Cylinder   Cone   Sphere

a. $2\pi r^3 \div \dfrac{2}{3}\pi r^3 =$

b. $\dfrac{4}{3}\pi r^3 \div \dfrac{2}{3}\pi r^3 =$

c. $2\pi r^3 \div \dfrac{4}{3}\pi r^3 =$

Name_____ Date_____

9.4 Zero and Negative Exponents (continued)

3 ACTIVITY: Writing a Definition

Work with a partner.

Compare the two methods used to simplify $\dfrac{3^2}{3^5}$. Then describe how you can rewrite a power with a negative exponent as a fraction.

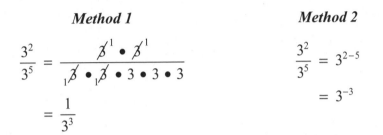

Method 1

$$\frac{3^2}{3^5} = \frac{\cancel{3}^1 \cdot \cancel{3}^1}{{}_1\cancel{3} \cdot {}_1\cancel{3} \cdot 3 \cdot 3 \cdot 3}$$

$$= \frac{1}{3^3}$$

Method 2

$$\frac{3^2}{3^5} = 3^{2-5}$$

$$= 3^{-3}$$

What Is Your Answer?

4. **IN YOUR OWN WORDS** How can you define zero and negative exponents? Give two examples of each.

Name _____ Date _____

Evaluate the expression.

1. 29^0

2. 12^{-1}

3. $(-15)^{-2} \bullet (-15)^2$

4. $10^{-4} \bullet 10^{-6}$

5. $\dfrac{1}{3^{-3}} \bullet \dfrac{1}{3^5}$

6. $\dfrac{(4.1)^8}{(4.1)^5 \bullet (4.1)^7}$

Simplify. Write the expression using only positive exponents.

7. $19x^{-6}$

8. $\dfrac{14a^{-5}}{a^{-8}}$

9. $\dfrac{16y^4}{4y^{10}}$

10. $3t^6 \bullet 8t^{-6}$

11. $7k^{-2} \bullet 5m^0 \bullet k^9$

12. $\dfrac{12s^{-1} \bullet 4^{-2} \bullet r^3}{s^2 \bullet r^5}$

13. The density of a proton is about $\dfrac{1.64 \times 10^{-24}}{3.7 \times 10^{-38}}$ grams per cubic centimeter. Simplify the expression.

Name_____ Date_____

9.5 Reading Scientific Notation
For use with Activity 9.5

Essential Question How can you read numbers that are written in scientific notation?

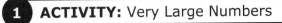

1 ACTIVITY: Very Large Numbers

Work with a partner.

- Use a calculator. Experiment with multiplying large numbers until your calculator gives an answer that is *not* in standard form.

- When the calculator on the right was used to multiply 2 billion by 3 billion, it listed the result as

$$6.0\text{E}+18.$$

- Multiply 2 billion by 3 billion by hand. Use the result to explain what $6.0\text{E}+18$. means.

- Check your explanation using products of other large numbers.

- Why didn't the calculator show the answer in standard form?

- Experiment to find the maximum number of digits your calculator displays. For instance, if you multiply 1000 by 1000 and your calculator shows 1,000,000, then it can display 7 digits.

9.5 **Reading Scientific Notation** (continued)

2 ACTIVITY: Very Small Numbers

Work with a partner.

- Use a calculator. Experiment with multiplying very small numbers until your calculator gives an answer that is *not* in standard form.

- When the calculator at the right was used to multiply 2 billionths by 3 billionths, it listed the result as

  $$6.0\text{E}{-}18.$$

- Multiply 2 billionths by 3 billionths by hand. Use the result to explain what $6.0\text{E}{-}18$. means.

- Check your explanation using products of other very small numbers.

3 ACTIVITY: Reading Scientific Notation

Work with a partner.

Each description gives an example of a number written in scientific notation. Answer the question in the description. Write your answer in standard form.

a. Nearly 1.0×10^5 dust mites can live in 1 square yard of carpet.

How many dust mites can live in 100 square yards of carpet?

b. A micron is about 4.0×10^{-5} inch. The length of a dust mite is 250 microns.

How long is a dust mite in inches?

9.5 Reading Scientific Notation (continued)

c. About 1.0×10^{15} bacteria live in a human body.

How many bacteria are living in the humans in your classroom?

d. A micron is about 4.0×10^{-5} inch. The length of a bacterium is about 0.5 micron.

How many bacteria could lie end-to-end on your finger?

e. Earth has only about 1.5×10^8 kilograms of gold. Earth has a mass of 6.0×10^{24} kilograms.

What percent of Earth's mass is gold?

f. A gram is about 0.035 ounce. An atom of gold weighs about 3.3×10^{-22} gram.

How many atoms are in an ounce of gold?

What Is Your Answer?

4. IN YOUR OWN WORDS How can you read numbers that are written in scientific notation? Why do you think this type of notation is called "scientific notation?" Why is scientific notation important?

9.5 Practice
For use after Lesson 9.5

Tell whether the number is written in scientific notation. Explain.

1. 14×10^8

2. 2.6×10^{12}

3. 4.79×10^{-8}

4. 3.99×10^{16}

5. 0.15×10^{22}

6. 6×10^3

Write the number in standard form.

7. 4×10^9

8. 2×10^{-5}

9. 3.7×10^6

10. 4.12×10^{-3}

11. 7.62×10^{10}

12. 9.908×10^{-12}

13. Light travels at 3×10^8 meters per second.

   a. Write the speed of light in standard form.

   b. How far has light traveled after 5 seconds?

Name_____ Date_____

9.6 Writing Scientific Notation
For use with Activity 9.6

Essential Question How can you write a number in scientific notation?

1 **ACTIVITY:** Finding pH Levels

Work with a partner. In chemistry, pH is a measure of the activity of dissolved hydrogen ions (H^+). Liquids with low pH values are called acids. Liquids with high pH values are called bases.

Find the pH of each liquid. Is the liquid a base, neutral, or an acid?

a. Lime juice: $[H^+] = 0.01$

b. Egg: $[H^+] = 0.00000001$

c. Distilled water: $[H^+] = 0.0000001$

d. Ammonia water:
$[H^+] = 0.00000000001$

e. Tomato juice: $[H^+] = 0.0001$

f. Hydrochloric acid: $[H^+] = 1$

pH	$[H^+]$	
14	1×10^{-14}	
13	1×10^{-13}	
12	1×10^{-12}	Bases
11	1×10^{-11}	
10	1×10^{-10}	
9	1×10^{-9}	
8	1×10^{-8}	
7	1×10^{-7}	**Neutral**
6	1×10^{-6}	
5	1×10^{-5}	
4	1×10^{-4}	
3	1×10^{-3}	Acids
2	1×10^{-2}	
1	1×10^{-1}	
0	1×10^{0}	

9.6 **Writing Scientific Notation** (continued)

2 **ACTIVITY:** Writing Scientific Notation

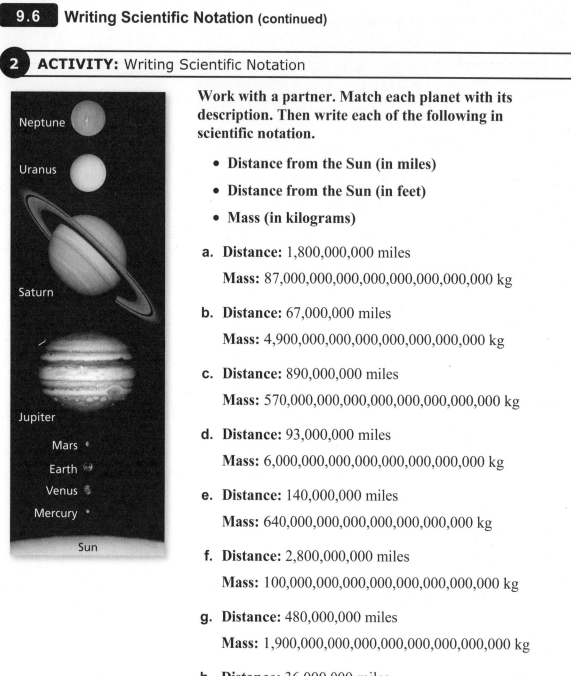

Work with a partner. Match each planet with its description. Then write each of the following in scientific notation.

- **Distance from the Sun (in miles)**
- **Distance from the Sun (in feet)**
- **Mass (in kilograms)**

a. Distance: 1,800,000,000 miles

Mass: 87,000,000,000,000,000,000,000,000 kg

b. Distance: 67,000,000 miles

Mass: 4,900,000,000,000,000,000,000,000 kg

c. Distance: 890,000,000 miles

Mass: 570,000,000,000,000,000,000,000,000 kg

d. Distance: 93,000,000 miles

Mass: 6,000,000,000,000,000,000,000,000 kg

e. Distance: 140,000,000 miles

Mass: 640,000,000,000,000,000,000,000 kg

f. Distance: 2,800,000,000 miles

Mass: 100,000,000,000,000,000,000,000,000 kg

g. Distance: 480,000,000 miles

Mass: 1,900,000,000,000,000,000,000,000,000 kg

h. Distance: 36,000,000 miles

Mass: 330,000,000,000,000,000,000,000 kg

Name_____ Date _____

9.6 Writing Scientific Notation (continued)

3 ACTIVITY: Making a Scale Drawing

Work with a partner. The illustration in Activity 2 is not drawn to scale.
Make a scale drawing of the distances in our solar system.

- Cut a sheet of paper into three strips of equal width. Tape the strips together.

- Draw a long number line. Label the number line in hundreds of millions of miles.

- Locate each planet's position on the number line.

What Is Your Answer?

4. **IN YOUR OWN WORDS** How can you write a number in scientific notation?

Name _____ Date _____

Write the number in scientific notation.

1. 4,200,000

2. 0.038

3. 600,000

4. 0.0000808

5. 0.0007

6. 29,010,000,000

Multiply. Write your answer in scientific notation.

7. $\left(6 \times 10^8\right) \times \left(4 \times 10^6\right)$

8. $\left(9 \times 10^{-3}\right) \times \left(9 \times 10^{-3}\right)$

9. $\left(7 \times 10^{-7}\right) \times \left(5 \times 10^{10}\right)$

10. $\left(1.4 \times 10^{-2}\right) \times \left(2 \times 10^{-15}\right)$

11. A patient has 0.0000075 gram of iron in 1 liter of blood. The normal level is between 6×10^{-7} gram and 1.6×10^{-5} gram. Is the patient's iron level normal? Write the patient's amount of iron in scientific notation.

Name_____ Date_____

9.6b Practice
For use after Lesson 9.6b

Add or subtract. Write your answer in scientific notation.

1. $\left(2 \times 10^4\right) + \left(7.2 \times 10^4\right)$

2. $\left(3.2 \times 10^{-2}\right) + \left(9.4 \times 10^{-2}\right)$

3. $\left(6.7 \times 10^5\right) - \left(4.3 \times 10^5\right)$

4. $\left(8.9 \times 10^{-3}\right) - \left(1.9 \times 10^{-3}\right)$

5. $\left(9.3 \times 10^8\right) + \left(8.6 \times 10^7\right)$

6. $\left(4.2 \times 10^3\right) + \left(2.7 \times 10^{-1}\right)$

7. $\left(1.4 \times 10^6\right) - \left(5.5 \times 10^5\right)$

8. $\left(1.9 \times 10^{-2}\right) - \left(3.1 \times 10^{-3}\right)$

Name _____ Date _____

Divide. Write your answer in scientific notation.

9. $\dfrac{8 \times 10^3}{2 \times 10^2}$

10. $\dfrac{2.34 \times 10^5}{7.8 \times 10^5}$

11. $\dfrac{3.4 \times 10^{-4}}{8.5 \times 10^2}$

12. $\dfrac{6.9 \times 10^{-7}}{4.6 \times 10^{-2}}$

13. How many times greater is the radius of a basketball than the radius of a marble?

Radius = 1.143×10^1 cm   Radius = 5×10^{-1} cm

Name_____ Date_____

Fair Game Review

The points represent vertices of a polygon. Graph the polygon in a coordinate plane. Then identify the polygon.

1. $J(-2, 0), K(-2, 4), L(3, 4), M(3, 0)$ 2. $A(-3, 2), B(0, -4), C(-4, -2)$

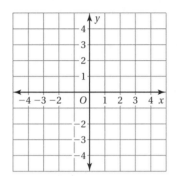

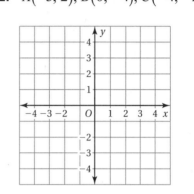

3. $W(-1, -2), X(-2, 1), Y(1, 4), Z(2, 1)$ 4. $D(1, -1), E(4, -1), F(4, -4), G(3, -4)$

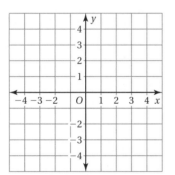

Additional Topics   **Fair Game Review** (continued)

Find the area.

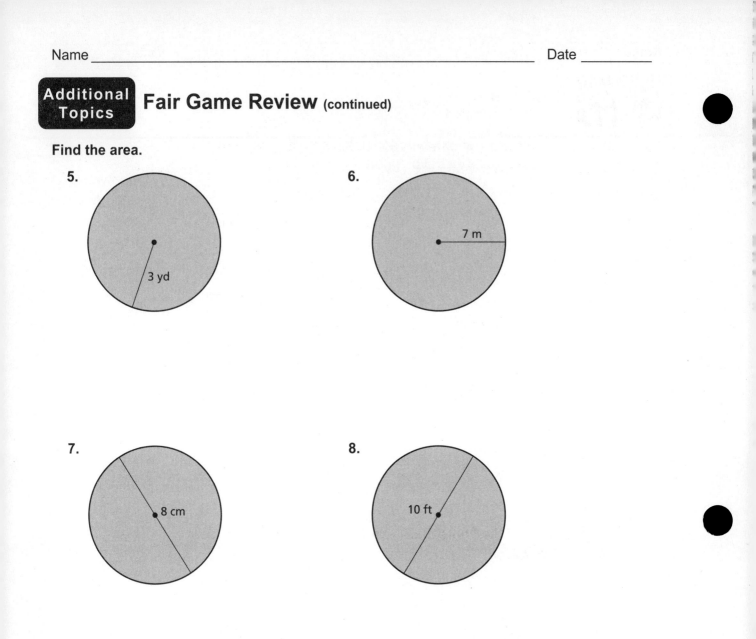

5.

3 yd

6.

7 m

7.

8 cm

8.

10 ft

9. A circular dog license has a diameter of 28 millimeters. What is the area of the dog license?

Name_____ Date_____

The vertices of a parallelogram are $A(-6, -1)$, $B(-3, 2)$, $C(3, 2)$, and $D(0, -1)$.
Draw the parallelogram and its image after the translation. Find the coordinates
of the image.

1. 4 units right and 2 units down

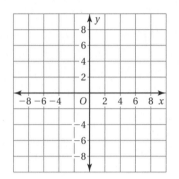

2. 2 units left and 1 unit up

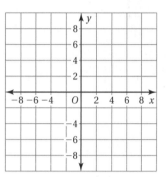

Find the coordinates of the figure after (a) reflecting in the *x*-axis and
(b) reflecting in the *y*-axis.

3. $W(-6, 1)$, $X(-6, 4)$, $Y(-2, 4)$, $Z(-2, 1)$

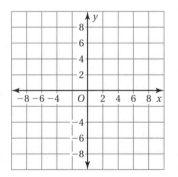

4. $P(4, -6)$, $Q(4, -1)$, $R(9, -6)$

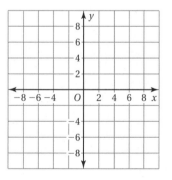

Topic 1 Practice (continued)

The vertices of a triangle are $L(-3, 1)$, $M(-3, 4)$, and $N(-1, 1)$. Rotate the triangle as described. Find the coordinates of the image.

5. 180° clockwise about the origin

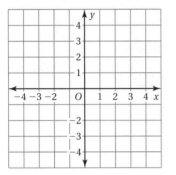

6. 90° counterclockwise about the origin

The vertices of a kite are $F(-6, -1)$, $G(-4, 1)$, $H(-2, -1)$, and $J(-4, -5)$. Dilate the kite using the given scale factor. Find the coordinates of the image. Identify the type of dilation.

7. scale factor = 2

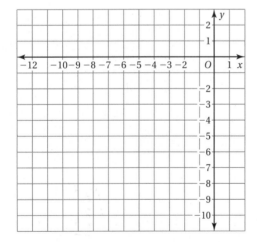

8. scale factor = $\dfrac{1}{2}$

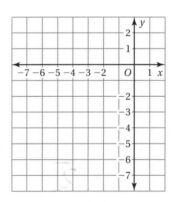

Topic 2

Practice
For use after Topic 2

Find the volume of the solid. Round your answer to the nearest tenth.

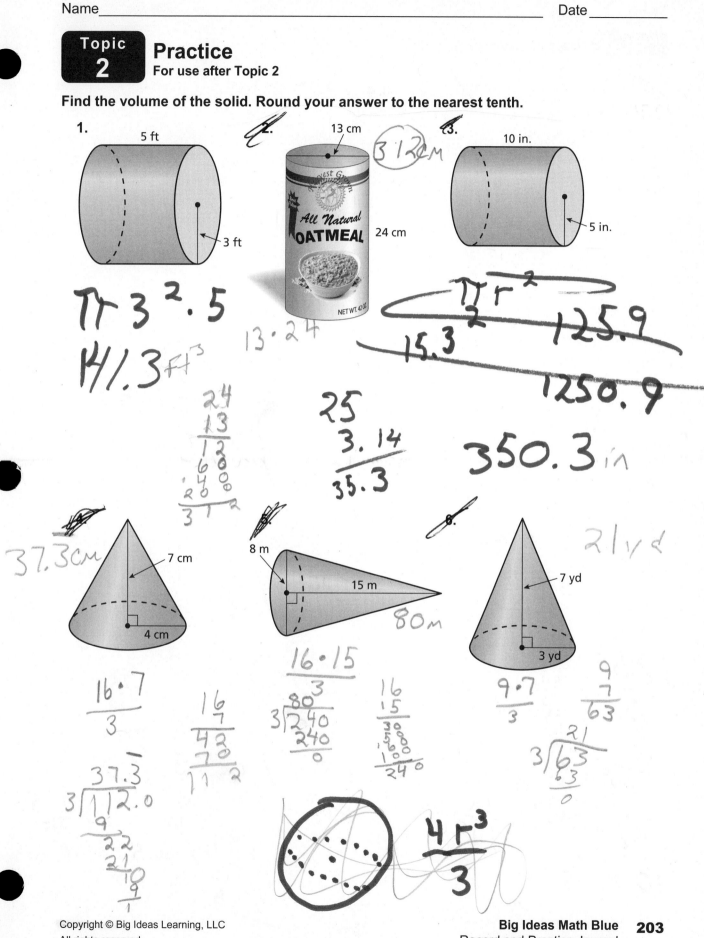

1.
5 ft
3 ft

$\pi 3^2 \cdot 5$
$141.3 ft^3$

2.
13 cm
24 cm
312 cm

$13 \cdot 24$

24
13
____
72
240
____
312

25
3.14
____
35.3

3.
10 in.
5 in.

$\frac{\pi r^2}{2}$
15.3
125.9
1250.9
350.3 in

4.
37.3 cm
7 cm
4 cm

$\frac{16 \cdot 7}{3}$

37.3
3)112.0
9
22
21
10
9
1

16
7
____
42
7
____
112

5.
8 m
15 m
80 m

$\frac{16 \cdot 15}{3}$

16
15
____
80
160
100
____
240

3)80
240
240
0

6.
7 yd
3 yd
21 yd

$\frac{9 \cdot 7}{3}$

9
7
____
63

3)63
63
0

21

9
7
____
63

$\frac{4r^3}{3}$

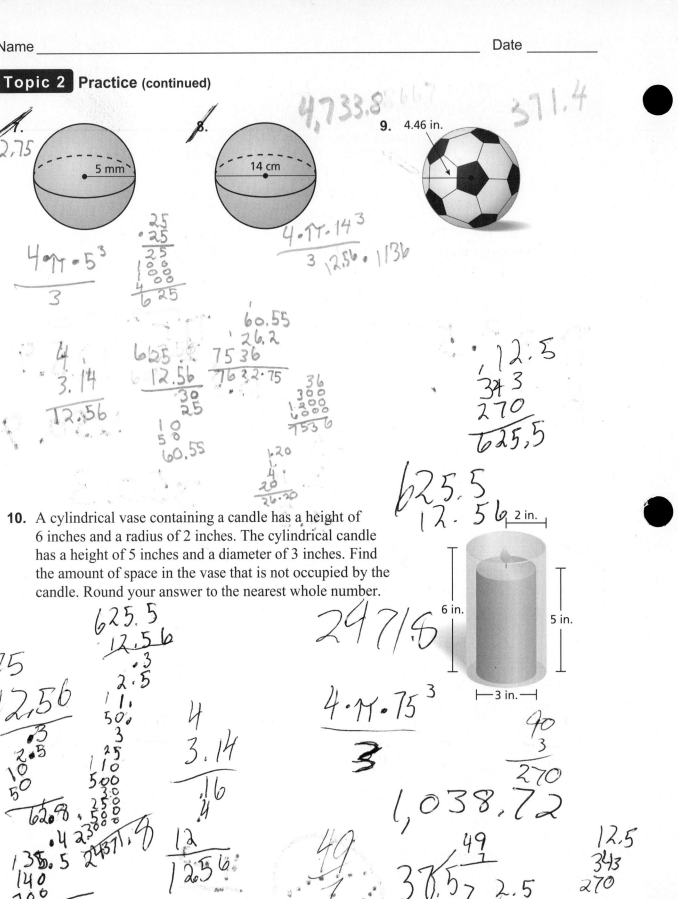

4,733.8 667   371.4

7622.75

$\frac{4 \cdot \pi \cdot 5^3}{3}$

$\frac{4 \cdot \pi \cdot 14^3}{3}$ 12.56 · 1136

10. A cylindrical vase containing a candle has a height of 6 inches and a radius of 2 inches. The cylindrical candle has a height of 5 inches and a diameter of 3 inches. Find the amount of space in the vase that is not occupied by the candle. Round your answer to the nearest whole number.

2471.8

$\frac{4 \cdot \pi \cdot 75^3}{3}$

1,038.72

Glossary

This student friendly glossary is designed to be a reference for key vocabulary, properties, and mathematical terms. Several of the entries include a short example to aid your understanding of important concepts.

Also available at BigIdeasMath.com:

- multi-language glossary
- vocabulary flash cards

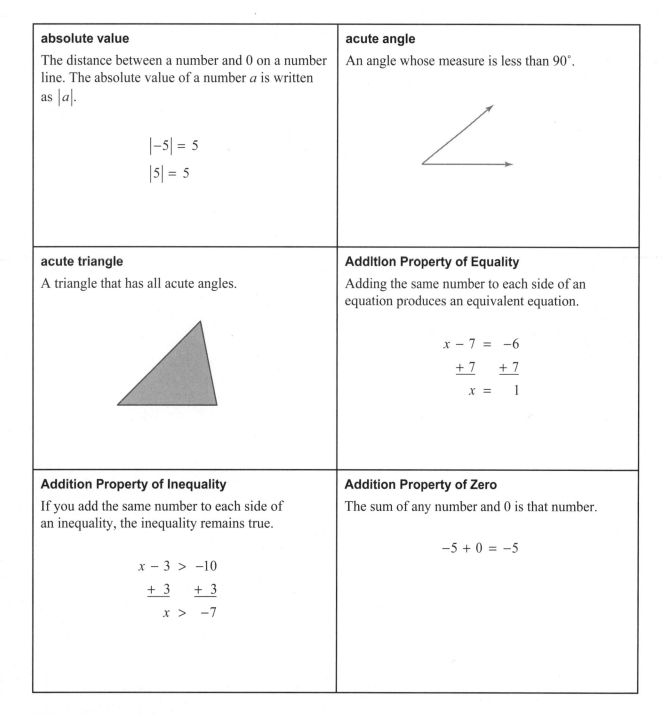

absolute value

The distance between a number and 0 on a number line. The absolute value of a number a is written as $|a|$.

$$|-5| = 5$$
$$|5| = 5$$

acute angle

An angle whose measure is less than 90°.

acute triangle

A triangle that has all acute angles.

Addition Property of Equality

Adding the same number to each side of an equation produces an equivalent equation.

$$x - 7 = -6$$
$$\underline{+\ 7 \quad\ +\ 7}$$
$$x = \quad 1$$

Addition Property of Inequality

If you add the same number to each side of an inequality, the inequality remains true.

$$x - 3 > -10$$
$$\underline{+\ 3 \quad\ +\ 3}$$
$$x > \quad -7$$

Addition Property of Zero

The sum of any number and 0 is that number.

$$-5 + 0 = -5$$

angle A figure formed by two rays with the same endpoint. 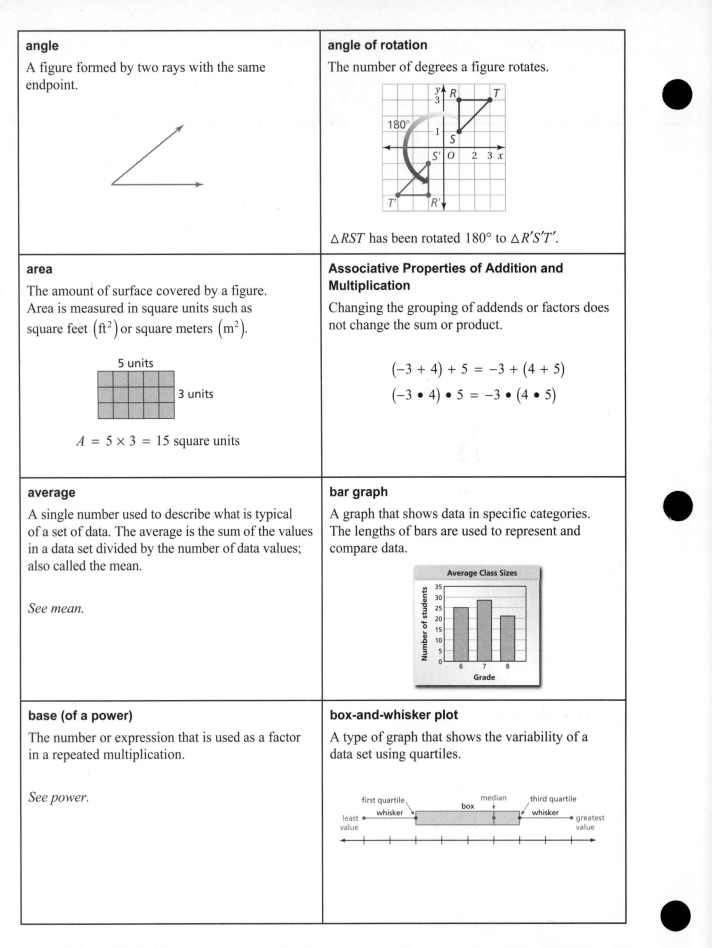	**angle of rotation** The number of degrees a figure rotates. $\triangle RST$ has been rotated $180°$ to $\triangle R'S'T'$.
area The amount of surface covered by a figure. Area is measured in square units such as square feet (ft^2) or square meters (m^2). 5 units 3 units $A = 5 \times 3 = 15$ square units	**Associative Properties of Addition and Multiplication** Changing the grouping of addends or factors does not change the sum or product. $$(-3 + 4) + 5 = -3 + (4 + 5)$$ $$(-3 \bullet 4) \bullet 5 = -3 \bullet (4 \bullet 5)$$
average A single number used to describe what is typical of a set of data. The average is the sum of the values in a data set divided by the number of data values; also called the mean. *See mean.*	**bar graph** A graph that shows data in specific categories. The lengths of bars are used to represent and compare data.
base (of a power) The number or expression that is used as a factor in a repeated multiplication. *See power.*	**box-and-whisker plot** A type of graph that shows the variability of a data set using quartiles.

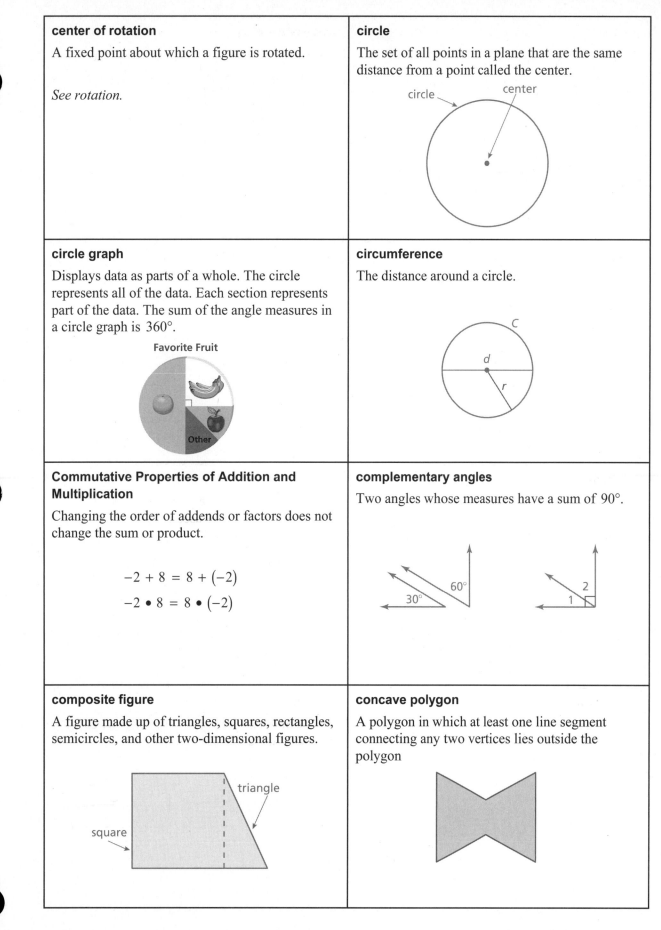

center of rotation

A fixed point about which a figure is rotated.

See rotation.

circle

The set of all points in a plane that are the same distance from a point called the center.

circle graph

Displays data as parts of a whole. The circle represents all of the data. Each section represents part of the data. The sum of the angle measures in a circle graph is 360°.

Favorite Fruit

circumference

The distance around a circle.

Commutative Properties of Addition and Multiplication

Changing the order of addends or factors does not change the sum or product.

$$-2 + 8 = 8 + (-2)$$
$$-2 \bullet 8 = 8 \bullet (-2)$$

complementary angles

Two angles whose measures have a sum of 90°.

composite figure

A figure made up of triangles, squares, rectangles, semicircles, and other two-dimensional figures.

concave polygon

A polygon in which at least one line segment connecting any two vertices lies outside the polygon

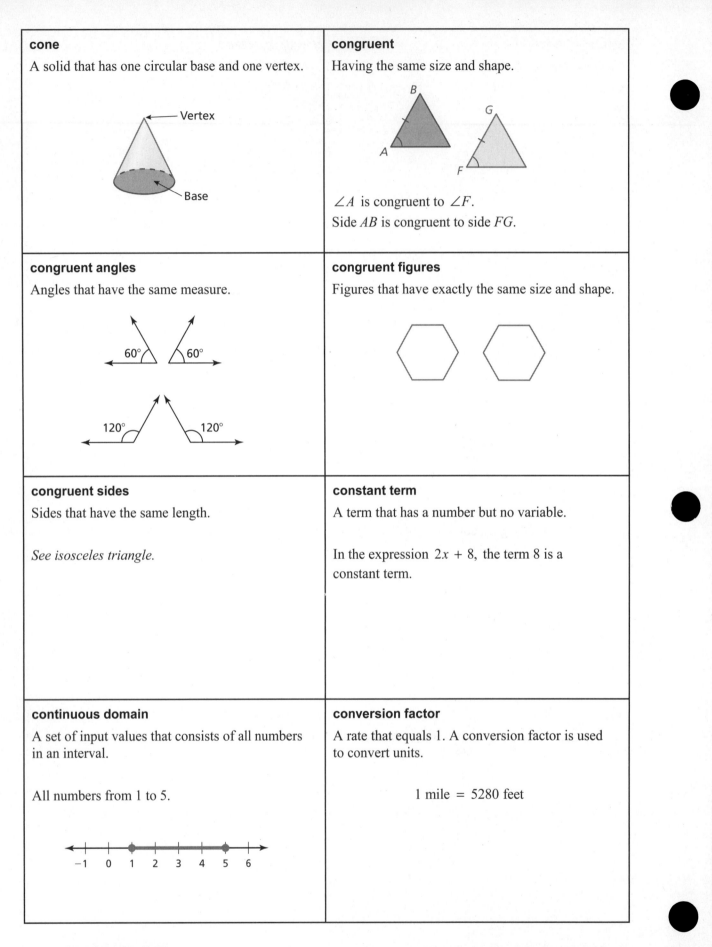

cone

A solid that has one circular base and one vertex.

Vertex

Base

congruent

Having the same size and shape.

$\angle A$ is congruent to $\angle F$.

Side AB is congruent to side FG.

congruent angles

Angles that have the same measure.

60°   60°

120°   120°

congruent figures

Figures that have exactly the same size and shape.

congruent sides

Sides that have the same length.

See isosceles triangle.

constant term

A term that has a number but no variable.

In the expression $2x + 8$, the term 8 is a constant term.

continuous domain

A set of input values that consists of all numbers in an interval.

All numbers from 1 to 5.

−1 0 1 2 3 4 5 6

conversion factor

A rate that equals 1. A conversion factor is used to convert units.

1 mile = 5280 feet

convex polygon	**coordinate plane**
A polygon in which every line segment connecting any two vertices lies entirely inside the polygon.	A coordinate plane is formed by the intersection of a horizontal number line, usually called the *x*-axis, and a vertical number line, usually called the *y*-axis.
cube	**cube(d)**
A rectangular prism with 6 congruent square faces.	A number cubed is the number raised to the third power. 2 cubed means 2^3, or 8.
cube root	**cylinder**
A number that when multiplied by itself, and then multiplied by itself again, equals the given number. The cube root of −27 is −3.	A solid that has two parallel, congruent circular bases.
data	**decimal**
Information, often given in the form of numbers or facts.	A number that is written using the base-ten place value system. Each place value is ten times the place value to the right. The decimal 2.15 represents 2 ones plus 1 tenth plus 5 hundredths, or two and fifteen hundredths.

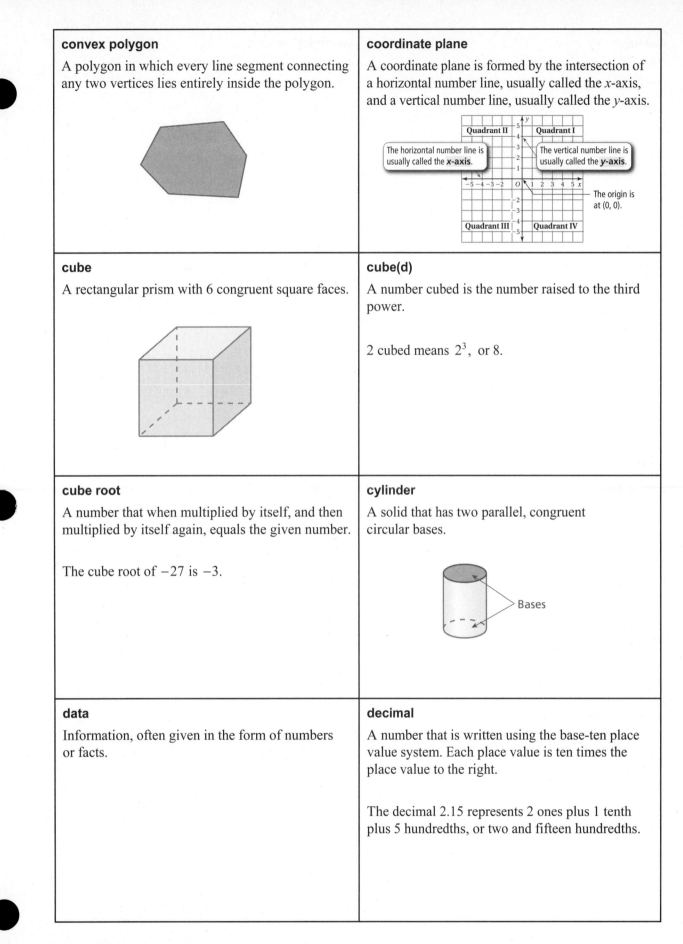

degree	**diameter (of a circle)**
A unit used to measure angles.	The distance across a circle through the center.
$90°$, $45°$, $32°$	*See circumference.*

difference	**dilation**
The result when one number is subtracted from another number.	A transformation in which a figure is made larger or smaller with respect to a fixed point called the center of dilation.
The difference of 4 and -3 is $4 - (-3)$, or 7.	$A'B'C'$ is a dilation of ABC with respect to the origin. The scale factor is 2.

direct variation	**discrete domain**
Two quantities x and y show direct variation when $y = kx$, where k is a number and $k \neq 0$.	A set of input values that consists of only certain numbers in an interval.
The graph is a line that passes through the origin.	Integers from 1 to 5.

Distributive Property	**Division Property of Equality**
To multiply a sum or difference by a number, multiply each number in the sum or difference by the number outside the parentheses. Then evaluate.	Dividing each side of an equation by the same number produces an equivalent equation
$3(2 + 9) = 3(2) + 3(9)$ $3(2 - 9) = 3(2) - 3(9)$	$4x = -40$ $\dfrac{4x}{4} = \dfrac{-40}{4}$ $x = -10$

Division Property of Inequality	**domain**

Division Property of Inequality

If you divide each side of an inequality by the same positive number, the inequality remains true.

If you divide each side of an inequality by the same negative number, the inequality symbol must be reversed for the inequality to remain true.

$$4x > -12 \qquad\qquad -5x > 30$$

$$\frac{4x}{4} > \frac{-12}{4} \qquad\qquad \frac{-5x}{-5} < \frac{30}{-5}$$

$$x > -3 \qquad\qquad x < -6$$

domain

The set of all input values of a function.

For the ordered pairs $(0, 6)$, $(1, 7)$, $(2, 8)$, and $(3, 9)$, the domain is 0, 1, 2, and 3.

---

enlargement

A dilation with a scale factor greater than 1.

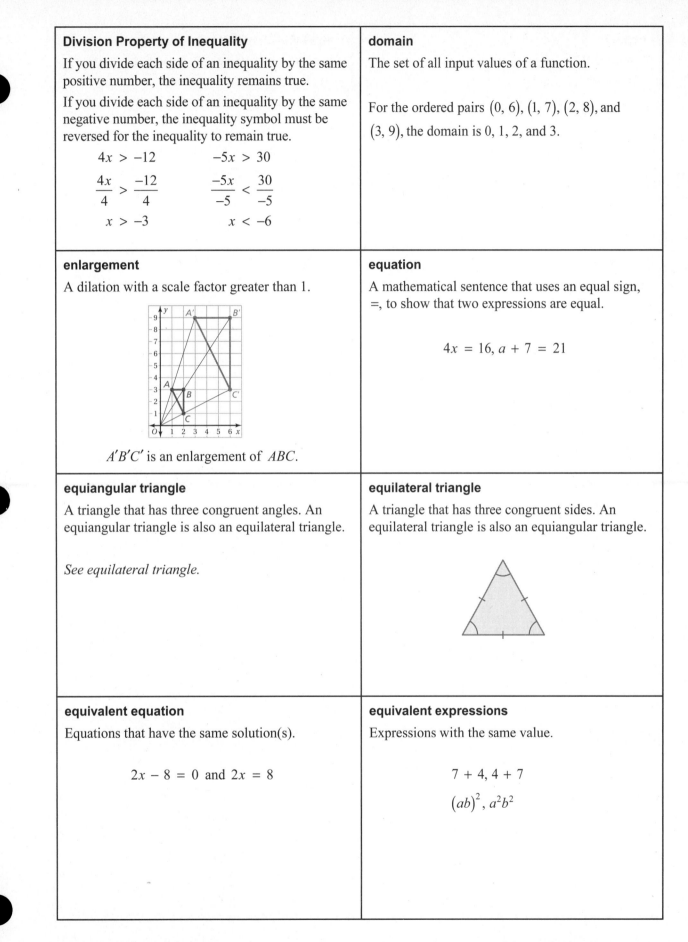

$A'B'C'$ is an enlargement of ABC.

equation

A mathematical sentence that uses an equal sign, =, to show that two expressions are equal.

$$4x = 16, \; a + 7 = 21$$

---

equiangular triangle

A triangle that has three congruent angles. An equiangular triangle is also an equilateral triangle.

See equilateral triangle.

equilateral triangle

A triangle that has three congruent sides. An equilateral triangle is also an equiangular triangle.

---

equivalent equation

Equations that have the same solution(s).

$$2x - 8 = 0 \text{ and } 2x = 8$$

equivalent expressions

Expressions with the same value.

$$7 + 4, \, 4 + 7$$

$$(ab)^2, \, a^2b^2$$

---

estimate

To find an approximate solution to a problem.

You can estimate the sum of $98 + 53$ as $100 + 50$, or 150.

evaluate (an algebraic expression)

Substitute a number for each variable in an algebraic expression. Then use the order of operations to find the value of the numerical expression.

$$\text{Evaluate } 3x + 5 \text{ when } x = 6.$$
$$3x + 5 = 3(6) + 5$$
$$= 18 + 5$$
$$= 23$$

exponent

The number of times a base is used as a factor in a repeated multiplication.

See power.

expression

A mathematical phrase containing numbers, operations, and/or variables.

$$12 + 6, 18 + 3 \times 4,$$
$$8 + x, 6 \times a - b$$

exterior angles

When two parallel lines are cut by a transversal, four exterior angles are formed on the outside of the parallel lines.

$\angle 3, \angle 4, \angle 5,$ and $\angle 6$ are interior angles.

$\angle 1, \angle 2, \angle 7,$ and $\angle 8$ are exterior angles.

factor

When whole numbers other than zero are multiplied together, each number is a factor of the product.

$2 \times 3 \times 4 = 24$, so 2, 3, and 4 are factors of 24.

formula

An equation that shows how one variable is related to one or more other variables.

$A = \ell w$ is the formula for the area of a rectangle.

fraction

A number in the form $\dfrac{a}{b}$, where $b \neq 0$.

$$\frac{1}{2}, \frac{5}{9}$$

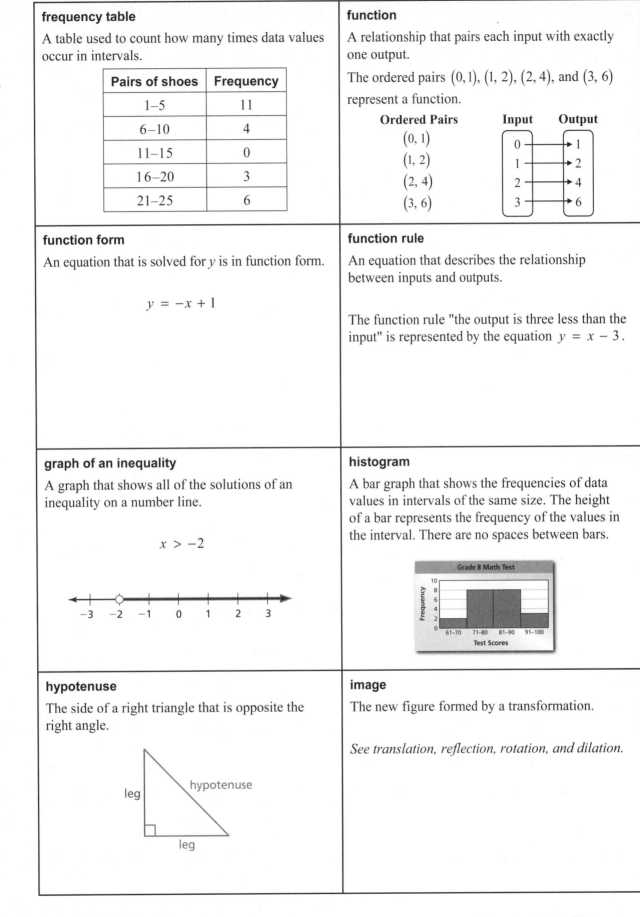

frequency table

A table used to count how many times data values occur in intervals.

Pairs of shoes	Frequency
1–5	11
6–10	4
11–15	0
16–20	3
21–25	6

function

A relationship that pairs each input with exactly one output.

The ordered pairs $(0, 1)$, $(1, 2)$, $(2, 4)$, and $(3, 6)$ represent a function.

Ordered Pairs	Input	Output
$(0, 1)$	0	1
$(1, 2)$	1	2
$(2, 4)$	2	4
$(3, 6)$	3	6

function form

An equation that is solved for y is in function form.

$$y = -x + 1$$

function rule

An equation that describes the relationship between inputs and outputs.

The function rule "the output is three less than the input" is represented by the equation $y = x - 3$.

graph of an inequality

A graph that shows all of the solutions of an inequality on a number line.

$$x > -2$$

histogram

A bar graph that shows the frequencies of data values in intervals of the same size. The height of a bar represents the frequency of the values in the interval. There are no spaces between bars.

hypotenuse

The side of a right triangle that is opposite the right angle.

image

The new figure formed by a transformation.

See translation, reflection, rotation, and dilation.

indirect measurement

Using similar figures to find a missing measurement that is difficult to find directly.

$$\frac{x}{60} = \frac{40}{50}$$

$$60 \bullet \frac{x}{60} = 60 \bullet \frac{40}{50}$$

$$x = 48$$

The distance across the river is 48 feet.

---

inductive

Making conclusions from several known cases.

---

inequality

A mathematical sentence that compares expressions. It contains the symbols $<, >, \leq,$ or $\geq$.

$$x - 4 < -14, \quad x + 5 \geq -67$$

---

input

A number on which a function operates.

See function.

---

input-output table

A table that lists the output of a function for each input.

Input, x	Output, y
1	3
2	4
3	5
4	6

---

integers

The set of whole numbers and their opposites.

$$\dots -3, -2, -1, 0, 1, 2, 3, \dots$$

---

interest

Money paid or earned for the use of money.

See simple interest.

---

interior angles

When two parallel lines are cut by a transversal, four interior angles are formed on the inside of the parallel lines.

See exterior angles.

---

inverse operations Operations that "undo" each other, such as addition and subtraction or multiplication and division.	**irrational number** A number that cannot be written as the ratio of two integers. $$\pi, \sqrt{14}$$
isosceles triangle A triangle that has at least two congruent sides. 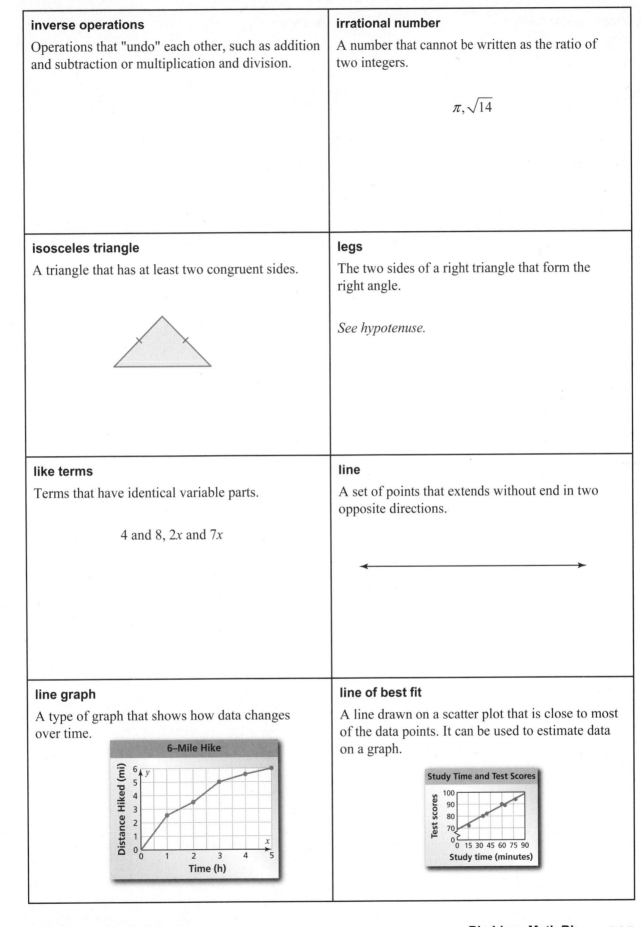	**legs** The two sides of a right triangle that form the right angle. *See hypotenuse.*
like terms Terms that have identical variable parts. 4 and 8, $2x$ and $7x$	**line** A set of points that extends without end in two opposite directions.
line graph A type of graph that shows how data changes over time.	**line of best fit** A line drawn on a scatter plot that is close to most of the data points. It can be used to estimate data on a graph.

line of reflection

A line that a figure is reflected in to create a mirror image of the original figure.

See reflection.

line plot

A type of graph that shows the number of times each value occurs in a data set.

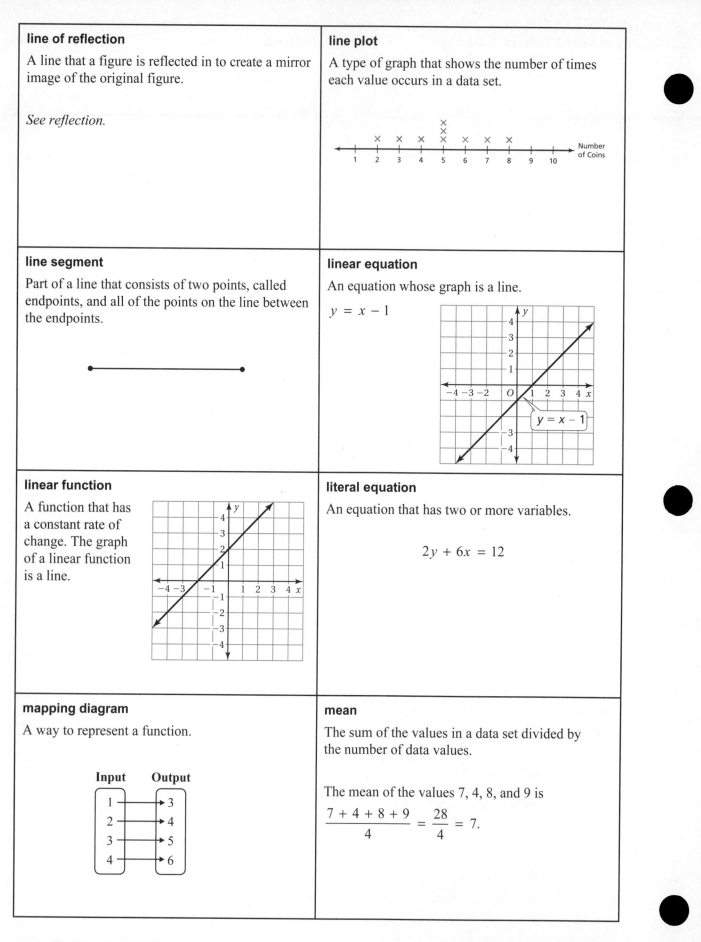

line segment

Part of a line that consists of two points, called endpoints, and all of the points on the line between the endpoints.

linear equation

An equation whose graph is a line.

$y = x - 1$

linear function

A function that has a constant rate of change. The graph of a linear function is a line.

literal equation

An equation that has two or more variables.

$$2y + 6x = 12$$

mapping diagram

A way to represent a function.

mean

The sum of the values in a data set divided by the number of data values.

The mean of the values 7, 4, 8, and 9 is

$$\frac{7 + 4 + 8 + 9}{4} = \frac{28}{4} = 7.$$

measure of central tendency

A measure that represents the center of a data set.

The mean, median, and mode are all measures of central tendency.

median

For a data set with an odd number of ordered values, the median is the middle data value. For a data set with an even number of ordered values, the median is the mean of the two middle values.

The median of the data set 24, 25, 29, 33, 38 is 29 because 29 is the middle value.

metric system

Decimal system of measurement, based on powers of 10, that contains units for length, capacity, and mass.

centimeter, meter, liter, kilogram

mode

The data value or values that occur most often. Data can have one mode, more than one mode, or no mode.

The modes of the data set 3, 4, 4, 7, 7, 9, 12 are 4 and 7 because they occur most often.

Multiplication Properties of Zero and One

The product of any number and 0 is 0.
The product of any number and 1 is that number.

$$-5 \bullet 0 = 0$$
$$-6 \bullet 1 = -6$$

Multiplication Property of Equality

Multiplying each side of an equation by the same number produces an equivalent equation.

$$-\frac{2}{3}x = 8$$
$$-\frac{3}{2} \bullet \left(-\frac{2}{3}x\right) = -\frac{3}{2} \bullet 8$$
$$x = -12$$

Multiplication Property of Inequality

If you multiply each side of an inequality by the same positive number, the inequality remains true.
If you multiply each side of an inequality by the same negative number, the direction of the inequality symbol must be reversed for the inequality to remain true.

$$\frac{x}{2} < -9 \qquad\qquad \frac{x}{-6} < 3$$
$$2 \bullet \frac{x}{2} < 2 \bullet (-9) \qquad -6 \bullet \frac{x}{-6} > -6 \bullet 3$$
$$x < -18 \qquad\qquad\qquad x > -18$$

negative number

A number less than 0.

$$-0.25, -10, -500$$

nonlinear function

A function that does not have a constant rate of change. The graph of a nonlinear function is not a line.

$y = x^3$

number line

A line whose points are associated with numbers that increase from left to right.

obtuse angle

An angle whose measure is greater than 90° and less than 180°.

obtuse triangle

A triangle that has one obtuse angle.

order of operations

The order in which to perform operations when evaluating expressions with more than one operation.

To evaluate $5 + 2 \times 3,$ you perform the multiplication before the addition.

ordered pair

A pair of numbers (x, y) used to locate a point in a coordinate plane. The first number is the x-coordinate, and the second number is the y-coordinate.

$(-2, 1)$

The x-coordinate of the point $(-2, 1)$ is $-2,$ and the y-coordinate is 1.

origin

The point, represented by the ordered pair $(0, 0),$ where the x-axis and the y-axis meet in a coordinate plane.

See coordinate plane.

outlier

A data value that is much greater or much less than the other values.

In the data set 23, 42, 33, 117, 36, and 40, the outlier is 117.

output

A number produced by evaluating a function using a given input.

See function.

parallel (lines)

Two lines in the same plane that do not intersect. Parallel lines have the same slope.

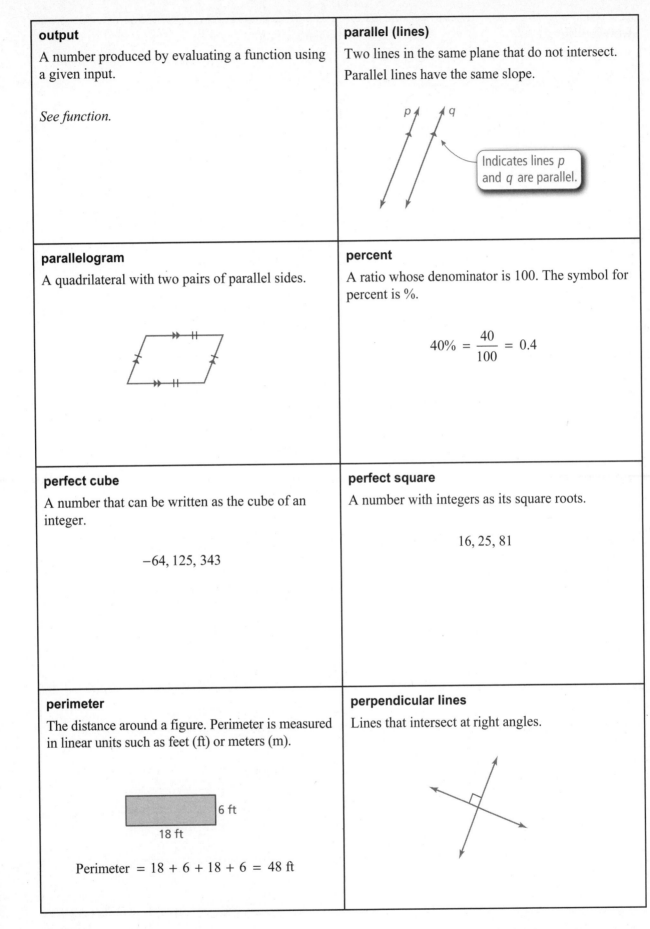

Indicates lines p and q are parallel.

parallelogram

A quadrilateral with two pairs of parallel sides.

percent

A ratio whose denominator is 100. The symbol for percent is %.

$$40\% = \frac{40}{100} = 0.4$$

perfect cube

A number that can be written as the cube of an integer.

$$-64, 125, 343$$

perfect square

A number with integers as its square roots.

$$16, 25, 81$$

perimeter

The distance around a figure. Perimeter is measured in linear units such as feet (ft) or meters (m).

6 ft

18 ft

Perimeter $= 18 + 6 + 18 + 6 = 48$ ft

perpendicular lines

Lines that intersect at right angles.

pictograph

A type of graph that shows data using pictures.

Number of Miles Biked

Monday	🚲 🚲
Tuesday	🚲 🚲 🚲
Wednesday	🚲 🚲
Thursday	🚲
Friday	🚲 🚲
Saturday	🚲 🚲 🚲 🚲 🚲

🚲 = 2 miles

plane

A flat surface that extends without end in all directions.

point

A position in space represented with a dot.

polygon

A closed plane figure made up of three or more line segments that intersect only at their endpoints.

vertex

positive number

A number greater than 0.

0.5, 2, 100

power

A product of repeated factors.

base   exponent

$$\left(\frac{1}{2}\right)^5 = \frac{1}{2} \bullet \frac{1}{2} \bullet \frac{1}{2} \bullet \frac{1}{2} \bullet \frac{1}{2}$$

Power $\frac{1}{2}$ is used as a factor 5 times.

prime factorization

A whole number written as the product of prime numbers.

The prime factorization of 60 is $2 \times 2 \times 3 \times 5$.

prism

A polyhedron that has two parallel, congruent bases. The other faces are parallelograms.

Base

Lateral face

product

The result when two or more numbers are multiplied.

The product of 4 and -3 is $4 \times (-3)$, or -12.

Product of Powers Property

To multiply powers with the same base, add their exponents.

$$3^7 \times 3^{10} = 3^{7+10} = 3^{17}$$

Product Property of Square Roots

$\sqrt{xy} = \sqrt{x} \bullet \sqrt{y}$, where $x, y \geq 0$

$$\sqrt{4 \bullet 3} = \sqrt{4} \bullet \sqrt{3} = 2\sqrt{3}$$

proportion

An equation stating that two ratios are equivalent.

$$\frac{3}{4} = \frac{12}{16}$$

protractor

A tool used to measure angles.

pyramid

A polyhedron that has one base. The other faces are triangles.

Lateral face

Base

Pythagorean Theorem

In any right triangle, the sum of the squares of the lengths of the legs is equal to the square of the length of the hypotenuse.

$$a^2 + b^2 = c^2$$

13 cm   5 cm   12 cm

$$5^2 + 12^2 = 13^2$$

Pythagorean triple

A set of three positive integers a, b, and c, where $a^2 + b^2 = c^2$.

Because $3^2 + 4^2 = 5^2$, 3, 4, and 5 is a Pythagorean triple.

quadrants

The four regions created by the intersection of the *x*-axis and the *y*-axis in a coordinate plane.

See coordinate plane.

quadrilateral

A polygon with four sides.

quartiles

Used to divide a data set into four equal parts. The median (second quartile) divides the data set into two halves. The median of the lower half is the first quartile. The median of the upper half is the third quartile.

See box-and-whisker plot.

quotient

The result of a division.

The quotient of 10 and -5 is $10 \div (-5)$, or -2.

Quotient of Powers Property

To divide powers with the same base, subtract their exponents.

$$\frac{9^7}{9^3} = 9^{7-3} = 9^4$$

Quotient Property of Square Roots

When $x \geq 0$ and $y > 0$, the square root of a quotient is equal to the quotient of the square roots of the numerator and denominator.

$$\sqrt{\frac{7}{9}} = \frac{\sqrt{7}}{\sqrt{9}} = \frac{\sqrt{7}}{3}$$

radical sign

The symbol $\sqrt{}$ which is used to represent a square root.

$$\sqrt{25} = 5$$
$$-\sqrt{49} = -7$$
$$\pm\sqrt{100} = \pm 10$$

radicand

The number under a radical sign.

The radicand of $\sqrt{25}$ is 25.

radius (of a circle)	**range**
The distance from the center of a circle to any point on the circle.	The set of all output values of a function.
See circumference.	For the ordered pairs (0, 6), (1, 7), (2, 8), and (3, 9), the range is 6, 7, 8, and 9.

range (of a data set)	**rate**
The difference between the greatest value and the least value of a data set. The range describes how spread out the data are.	A ratio of two quantities with different units.
The range of the data set 12, 16, 18, 22, 27, 35 is $35 - 12 = 23$.	You read 3 books every 2 weeks.

ratio	**rational number**
A comparison of two quantities using division. The ratio of a to b $(\text{where } b \neq 0)$ can be written as a to b, $a : b$, or $\dfrac{a}{b}$.	A number that can be written as the ratio of two integers, $\dfrac{a}{b}$, where a and b are integers and $b \neq 0$.
$4 \text{ to } 1, \ 4 : 1, \text{ or } \dfrac{4}{1}$	$3 = \dfrac{3}{1}, \qquad -\dfrac{2}{5} = \dfrac{-2}{5}$ $0.25 = \dfrac{1}{4}, \qquad 1\dfrac{1}{3} = \dfrac{4}{3}$

ray	**real number**
A part of a line that has one endpoint and extends without end in one direction.	The set of all rational and irrational numbers.
	$4, \ -6.5, \ \pi, \ \sqrt{14}$

reciprocals

Two numbers whose product is 1.

Because $\dfrac{4}{5} \times \dfrac{5}{4} = 1$, $\dfrac{4}{5}$ and $\dfrac{5}{4}$ are reciprocals.

rectangle

A parallelogram with four right angles.

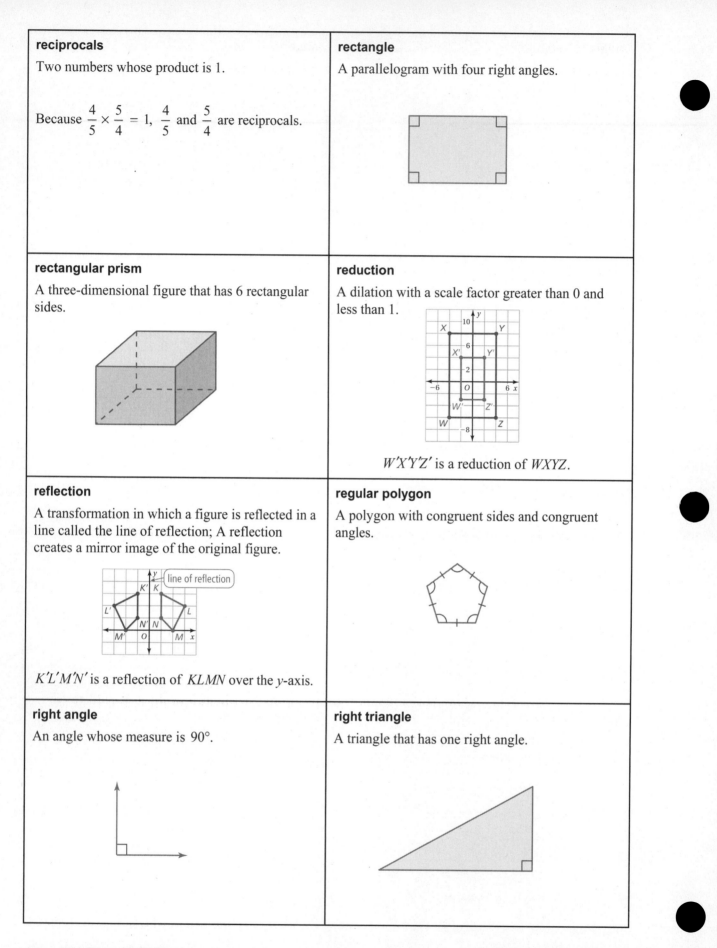

rectangular prism

A three-dimensional figure that has 6 rectangular sides.

reduction

A dilation with a scale factor greater than 0 and less than 1.

$W'X'Y'Z'$ is a reduction of $WXYZ$.

reflection

A transformation in which a figure is reflected in a line called the line of reflection; A reflection creates a mirror image of the original figure.

$K'L'M'N'$ is a reflection of $KLMN$ over the y-axis.

regular polygon

A polygon with congruent sides and congruent angles.

right angle

An angle whose measure is 90°.

right triangle

A triangle that has one right angle.

rise

The change in y between two points on a line.

See slope.

rotation

A transformation in which a figure is rotated about a point called the center of rotation; The number of degrees a figure rotates is the angle of rotation.

$\triangle RST$ has been rotated about the origin O to $\triangle R'S'T'$.

round

To approximate a number to a given place value.

132 rounded to the nearest ten is 130.

run

The change in x between two points on a line.

See slope.

sales tax

An additional amount of money charged on items by governments to raise money.

A 6% sales tax on a $20 item is
$20 \times 0.06 = \$1.20$.

scale factor

The ratio of the side lengths of the image of a dilation to the corresponding side lengths of the original figure.

See dilation.

scatter plot

A graph that shows the relationship between two data sets using ordered pairs in a coordinate plane.

scientific notation

A number is written in scientific notation when it is represented as the product of a factor and a power of 10. The factor must be at least 1 and less than 10.

$$8.3 \times 10^4$$
$$4 \times 10^{-3}$$

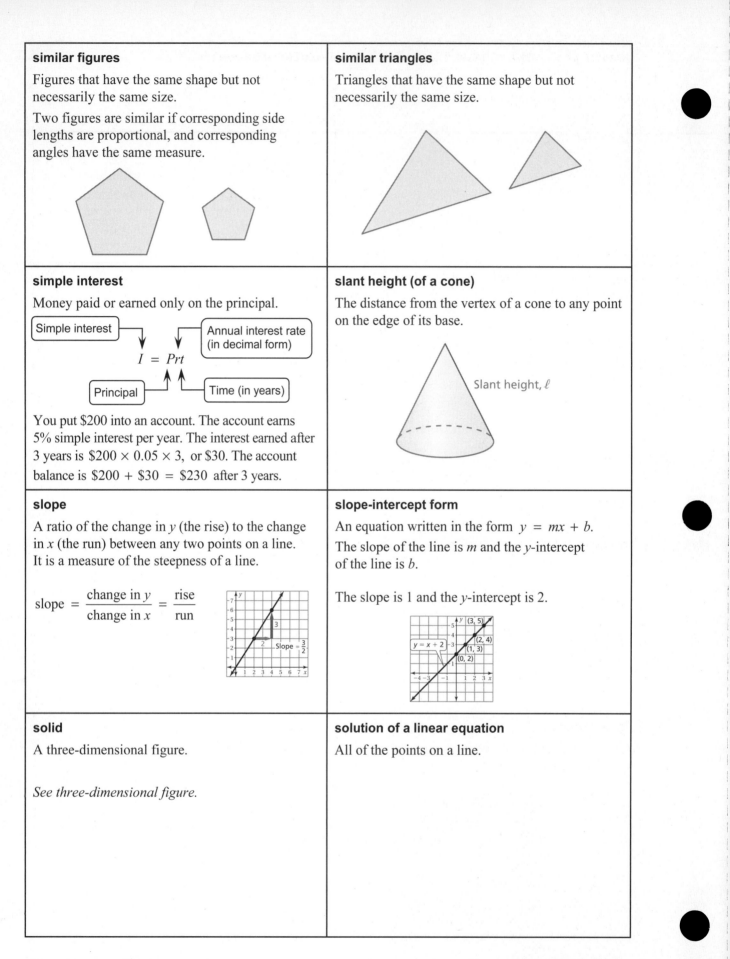

similar figures

Figures that have the same shape but not necessarily the same size.

Two figures are similar if corresponding side lengths are proportional, and corresponding angles have the same measure.

similar triangles

Triangles that have the same shape but not necessarily the same size.

simple interest

Money paid or earned only on the principal.

Simple interest → Annual interest rate (in decimal form)

$$I = Prt$$

Principal ↑ ↑ Time (in years)

You put $200 into an account. The account earns 5% simple interest per year. The interest earned after 3 years is $200 × 0.05 × 3, or $30. The account balance is $200 + $30 = $230 after 3 years.

slant height (of a cone)

The distance from the vertex of a cone to any point on the edge of its base.

Slant height, ℓ

slope

A ratio of the change in y (the rise) to the change in x (the run) between any two points on a line. It is a measure of the steepness of a line.

$$\text{slope} = \frac{\text{change in } y}{\text{change in } x} = \frac{\text{rise}}{\text{run}}$$

Slope = $\frac{3}{2}$

slope-intercept form

An equation written in the form $y = mx + b$.

The slope of the line is m and the y-intercept of the line is b.

The slope is 1 and the y-intercept is 2.

$y = x + 2$
(3, 5)
(2, 4)
(1, 3)
(0, 2)

solid

A three-dimensional figure.

See three-dimensional figure.

solution of a linear equation

All of the points on a line.

solution of a system of linear equations	**solution of an equation**
An ordered pair that makes each equation in a system of linear equations true. *See system of linear equations.*	A value that makes an equation true. 6 is the solution of the equation $x - 4 = 2$.
solution of an inequality	**solution set**
A value that makes an inequality true. A solution of the inequality $x + 3 > -9$ is $x = 2$.	The set of all solutions of an inequality.
sphere	**square**
The set of all points in three dimensions that are the same distance from a point called the center. The distance from the center to any point on the sphere is called the radius. center　　　　radius, r	A parallelogram with four right angles and four sides of equal length.
square root	**square(d)**
A number that when multiplied by itself, equals the given number. The two square roots of 100 are 10 and −10.	A number squared is the number raised to the second power. 5 squared means 5^2, or 25.

standard form

A linear equation written in the form $ax + by = c$, where a and b are not both zero.

$$-2x + 3y = -6$$

stem-and-leaf plot

A type of data display that orders numerical data and shows how they are distributed. Each data value is broken into a stem (digit or digits on the left) and a leaf (digit or digits on the right).

Test Scores

Stem	Leaf
6	6
7	2 7
8	1 1 3 4 4 6 8 8
9	0 0 0 2 7 8
10	0

Key: 9 | 4 = 94 points

straight angle

An angle whose measure is 180°.

Subtraction Property of Equality

Subtracting the same number from each side of an equation produces an equivalent equation.

$$\begin{aligned} x + 10 &= -12 \\ -10 & -10 \\ x &= -22 \end{aligned}$$

Subtraction Property of Inequality

If you subtract the same number from each side of an inequality, the inequality remains true.

$$\begin{aligned} x + 7 &> -20 \\ -7 & -7 \\ x &> -27 \end{aligned}$$

sum

The result when two or more numbers are added.

The sum of -4 and 3 is $-4 + 3$, or -1.

supplementary angles

Two angles whose measures have a sum of 180°.

surface area of a prism

The sum of the areas of all the faces of a prism.

$$\begin{aligned} S &= 2\ell w + 2\ell h + 2wh \\ &= 2(3)(5) + 2(3)(6) + 2(5)(6) \\ &= 30 + 36 + 60 \\ &= 126 \text{ in.}^2 \end{aligned}$$

6 in.
5 in.
3 in.

surface area of a solid

The sum of the areas of the outside surfaces of a solid.

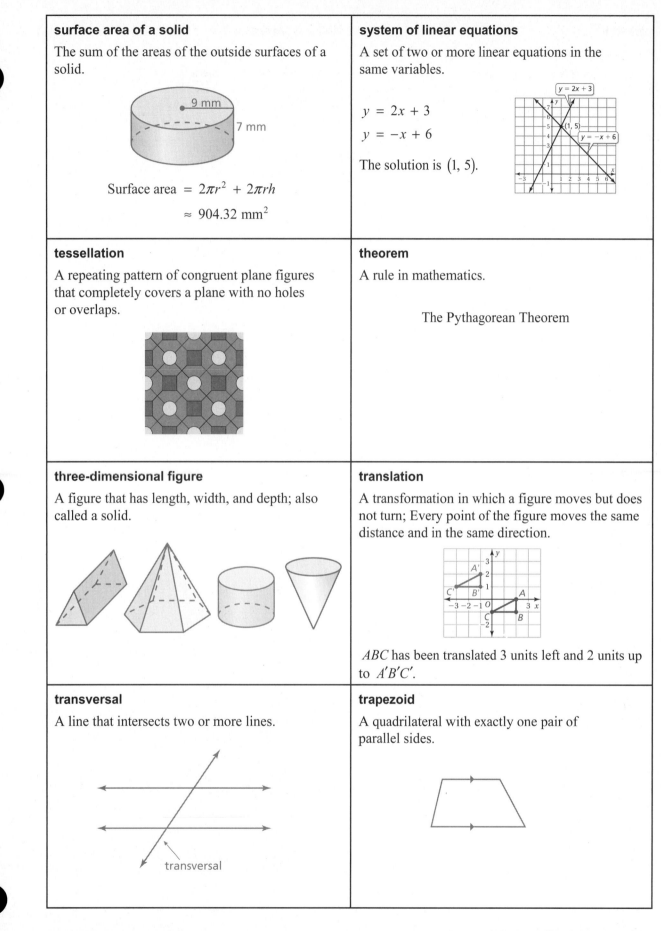

Surface area $= 2\pi r^2 + 2\pi rh$

$\approx 904.32 \text{ mm}^2$

system of linear equations

A set of two or more linear equations in the same variables.

$y = 2x + 3$

$y = -x + 6$

The solution is $(1, 5)$.

tessellation

A repeating pattern of congruent plane figures that completely covers a plane with no holes or overlaps.

theorem

A rule in mathematics.

The Pythagorean Theorem

three-dimensional figure

A figure that has length, width, and depth; also called a solid.

translation

A transformation in which a figure moves but does not turn; Every point of the figure moves the same distance and in the same direction.

ABC has been translated 3 units left and 2 units up to $A'B'C'$.

transversal

A line that intersects two or more lines.

transversal

trapezoid

A quadrilateral with exactly one pair of parallel sides.

triangle	two-way table
A polygon with three sides.	A table used to display two categories of data collected from the same source.

triangle

A polygon with three sides.

two-way table

A table used to display two categories of data collected from the same source.

		Football Game	
		Attend	**Not Attend**
Dance	**Attend**	35	5
	Not Attend	16	20

U.S. customary system

System of measurement that contains units for length, capacity, and weight.

  inches, feet, quarts, gallons, ounces, pounds

variable

A symbol, usually a letter, that represents one or more numbers.

x is a variable in $2x + 1$.

---

variable term

A term that has a variable.

In the expression $2x + 8$, the term $2x$ is a variable term.

vertex of a polygon

A point at which two sides of a polygon meet. The plural of vertex is vertices.

See polygon.

---

vertical angles

The angles opposite each other when two lines intersect. Vertical angles are congruent.

volume

A measure of the amount of space that a three-dimensional figure occupies. Volume is measured in cubic units such as cubic feet $\left(\text{ft}^3\right)$ or cubic meters $\left(\text{m}^3\right)$.

4 ft

3 ft

12 ft

Volume = $12 \bullet 3 \bullet 4 = 144 \text{ ft}^3$

---

whole number	***x*-axis**
The numbers 0, 1, 2, 3, 4, ….	The horizontal number line in a coordinate plane. *See coordinate plane.*

***x*-coordinate**	***x*-intercept**
The first coordinate in an ordered pair, which indicates how many units to move to the left or right from the origin. In the ordered pair $(3, 5)$, the *x*-coordinate is 3.	The *x*-coordinate of the point where a line crosses the *x*-axis.

***y*-axis**	***y*-coordinate**
The vertical number line in a coordinate plane. *See coordinate plane.*	The second coordinate in an ordered pair, which indicates how many units to move up or down from the origin. In the ordered pair $(3, 5)$, the *y*-coordinate is 5.

***y*-intercept**	
The *y*-coordinate of the point where a line crosses the *y*-axis. *See x-intercept.*	

Photo Credits

38 ©iStockphoto.com/Peter Finnie;
90 *left* ©iStockphoto.com/PeskyMonkey; *right*
©iStockphoto.com/shapecharge; **112** Estate Craft
Homes, Inc.; **121** ©ImageState; **130** Luminis;
147 Gina Brockett; **152** Larry Korhnak; **153** Photo by
Andy Newman; **176** ©iStockphoto.com/Franck Boston;
177 Stevyn Colgan; **191, 192** ©iStockphoto.com/
Kais Tolmats; **196** NASA

Cartoon Illustrations Tyler Stout

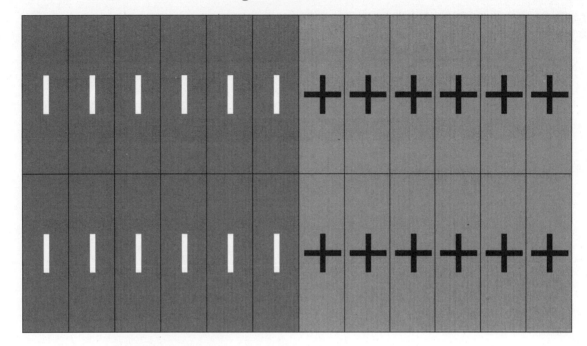

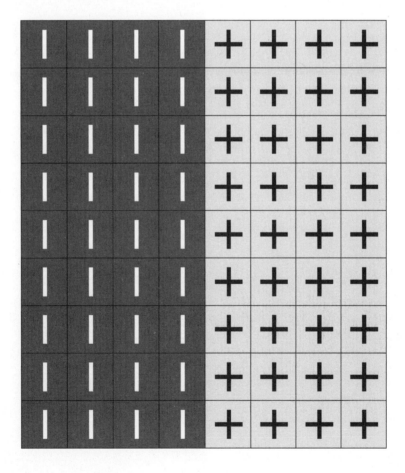